SUPER POWER SYNDROME

Also by Robert Jay Lifton

Who Owns Death: Capital
Punishment, the American Conscience,
and the End of Executions
(with Greg Mitchell)

Destroying the World to Save It: Aum
Shinrikyo, Apocalyptic Violence, and
the New Global Terrorism

Hiroshima in America: Fifty Years of
Denial (with Greg Mitchell)

The Protean Self: Human Resilience
in an Age of Fragmentation

The Genocidal Mentality: Nazi
Holocaust and Nuclear Threat
(with Eric Markusen)

The Future of Immortality—and
Other Essays for a Nuclear Age

The Nazi Doctors: Medical Killing
and the Psychology of Genocide

Indefensible Weapons: The Political
and Psychological Case Against
Nuclearism (with Richard Falk)

The Broken Connection: On Death
and the Continuity of Life

Six Lives/Six Deaths: Portraits from
Modern Japan (with Shuichi Kato
and Michael Reich)

The Life of the Self: Toward a New
Psychology

Living and Dying (with Eric Olson)

Home from the War: Vietnam
Veterans—Neither Victims nor
Executioners

Boundaries: Psychological Man in
Revolution

Death in Life: Survivors of Hiroshima

History and Human Survival: Essays
on the Young and the Old, Survivors
and the Dead, War and Peace, and
on Contemporary Psychohistory

Revolutionary Immortality: Mao
Tse-tung and the Chinese Cultural
Revolution

Thought Reform and the Psychology of
Totalism: A Study of "Brainwashing"
in China

Edited by Robert Jay Lifton

Beyond Invisible Walls: The Psychological Legacy of Soviet Trauma
(with Jacob D. Lindy)

In a Dark Time: Images for Survival
(with Nicholas Humphrey)

Last Aid: Medical Dimensions of
Nuclear War (with E. Chivian, S.
Chivian, and J.E. Mack)

Explorations in Psychohistory: The
Wellfleet Papers (with Eric Olson)

Crimes of War (with Richard Falk
and Gabriel Kolko)

America and the Asian Revolutions

The Woman in America

ABOUT THE AUTHOR

Robert Jay Lifton is Visiting Professor of Psychiatry at Harvard Medical School. He was previously Distinguished Professor of Psychiatry and Psychology at the Graduate School and Director of The Center on Violence and Human Survival at John Jay College of Criminal Justice at the City University of New York. Before that he held the Foundations' Fund Research Professorship of Psychiatry at Yale University for more than two decades.

He was an Air Force psychiatrist serving in the United States, Japan, and Korea from 1951-53. He was Research Associate in Psychiatry at Harvard from 1956-61, where he was affiliated with the Center for East Asian Studies, and prior to that was a Member of the Faculty of the Washington School of Psychiatry.

From mid-1995, he has been conducting psychological research on the problem of apocalyptic violence, focusing on Aum Shinrikyo, the extremist Japanese cult that released poison gas in Tokyo subways. His book *Destroying the World to Save It: Aum Shinrikyo, Apocalyptic Violence, and the New Global Terrorism* was published in 1999.

In many influential books and articles, he has examined Nazi doctors' killing in the name of healing and the psychology of genocide, nuclear weapons and their impact on death symbolism, Hiroshima survivors; Chinese thought reform and the Chinese Cultural Revolution, psychological trends in contemporary men and women, and the Vietnam War experience and Vietnam veterans. He has developed a general psychological perspective around the paradigm of death and the continuity of life and a stress upon symbolization and "formative process" and on the malleability of the contemporary or "protean" self. He is a winner of the National Book Award, the National Jewish Book Award, and the Los Angeles Times Book Prize.

SUPER POWER SYNDROME

AMERICA'S APOCALYPTIC CONFRONTATION WITH THE WORLD

ROBERT JAY LIFTON

Thunder's Mouth Press / Nation Books
New York

To my grandchildren
Dmitri, Jessica, Kimberly, and Lila

SUPERPOWER SYNDROME: *America's Apocalyptic Confrontation with the World*
Copyright © 2003 Robert Jay Lifton

Published by
Thunder's Mouth Press/Nation Books
245 West 17th St., 11th Floor
New York, NY 10011

Nation Books is a co-publishing venture of the Nation Institute
and Avalon Publishing Group Incorporated.

Library of Congress Cataloging-in-Publication Data is available.

ISBN 1-56025-512-9

9 8 7 6 5 4 3 2 1

Book design by Simon M. Sullivan
Printed in the United States of America
Distributed by Publishers Group West

CONTENTS

INTRODUCTION

I complete this book at a sad and dangerous moment in American history, and in world history as well. Our country, with the help of Great Britain, has ended the first phase of its war on Iraq: the phase of military victory. Iraq is in extraordinary chaos, and the occupiers have been highly uncertain about how best to set up arrangements for governing. As Americans we are confronted with two starkly contending narratives about the war. The first, put forward by the war planners, is that of a war to liberate the Iraqi people from a cruel dictator, the disarming of a dangerous regime (even if its weapons of mass destruction have not yet been found) to enable democracy to take root in the Middle East. The second is that of an invasion of Iraq by a foreign army—by an American superpower seeking to dominate the Middle East and the world at large, and now actively threatening other countries (Syria, Iran, North Korea) with a similar fate if they do not behave properly.

Certainly many Iraqis are happy to be free of a dictator who was murderous in the extreme. But that does not mean that they and other Islamics, along with much of the world, will not be deeply troubled by the second narrative: that of American superpower hegemony. That, in turn, could mean that an apparent military victory will be but the beginning of new violence, of profoundly harmful reverberations, of even perhaps the decline of the American superpower.

This has been a war of choice, one which our leaders have felt motivated to wage. While we claimed to be defenders of the United Nations (a number of whose resolutions Iraq had violated), we by no means fought a defensive war against someone else's aggression. Nor was it (in a newly favored American phrase) a "preemptive war," one fought in response to an attack an enemy has initiated or is in the process of initiating. Rather it was a *preventive* war, embarked upon because our leaders decided that, sometime in the future, Iraq could be dangerous to the United States. The "danger" that was "prevented," I will argue, was the impediment posed by Iraq and the power structure in the Middle East to American domination of that region and of the world itself; in other words, to a dream—an extreme, even apocalyptic one—cherished by our present leaders.

The doctrine of preventive war is at any time odious: it provides a rationale for anyone's murderous military ventures. But such a doctrine becomes especially grotesque in the nuclear age. We need to recall that, soon after the Soviet Union became a nuclear power, there were proposals in this country that we engage in a preventive war against it with the rationale that sometime in the future it might turn its nuclear weapons on us. Had we embarked on that preventive war, we would have killed millions or tens of millions of people in the Soviet Union, and, through the effects of radiation, millions more in various parts of the world.

We have to ask what is happening to our leaders and to us as a people when we reach the point of justifying a preventive war and taking pride in the fact that less than 200 Americans and British were killed in battle while thousands or perhaps tens of thousands of Iraqis died, or when we wallow in triumphalism—as though this had been a true contest between military equals and a glorious victory, rather than a slaughter as the world's most powerful military machine simply overwhelmed a relatively small and weak nation. No less disturbing, that triumphalism has been accompanied by widespread labeling of opponents of the war, or even those insufficiently enthusiastic about it, as "unpatriotic," "un-American," "traitors," or if they were in foreign countries "anti-American" and even "enemies" of America.

The invasion of Iraq followed upon the fanatical Islamist violence of September 11, 2001, and an American response that took the form of an amorphous "war on terror." That "war" is a manifestation of what I call "superpower syndrome," a medical metaphor meant to suggest aberrant behavior that is not just random but part of a more general psychological and political constellation. That constellation—the syndrome—developed in the aftermath of World War II but has recently taken an extreme, world-endangering form.

This book is an exploration, both psychological and historical, of how we reached our present predicament and how we might begin to extricate ourselves from it. It is my version of a patriotic act, an expression of deep concern for my country. Beneath its belligerence, I believe that country is now enmeshed in a landscape of fear. Yet we do possess a democratic tradition that allows for critical self-examination and constructive change in our national life.

CHAPTER I
THE APOCALYPTIC FACE-OFF

The apocalyptic imagination has spawned a new kind of violence at the beginning of the twenty-first century. We can, in fact, speak of a worldwide epidemic of violence aimed at massive destruction in the service of various visions of purification and renewal. In particular, we are experiencing what could be called an apocalyptic face-off between Islamist* forces, overtly visionary in their willingness to kill and die for their religion, and American forces claiming to be restrained and reasonable but no less visionary in their projection of a cleansing war-making and military power. Both sides are

*In keeping with general usage, *Islamist* refers to groups that are essentially theocratic and fundamentalist, and at times apocalyptic. *Islamic* is a more general ethnic as well as religious term for Muslims. The terms can of course overlap, and "Islamic state" can mean one run on Islamist principles.

energized by versions of intense idealism; both see themselves as embarked on a mission of combating evil in order to redeem and renew the world; and both are ready to release untold levels of violence to achieve that purpose.

The war on Iraq—a country with longstanding aspirations toward weapons of mass destruction but with no evident stockpiles of them and no apparent connection to the assaults of September 11—was a manifestation of that American visionary projection.

The religious fanaticism of Osama bin Laden and other Islamist zealots has, by now, a certain familiarity to us as to others elsewhere, for their violent demands for spiritual purification are aimed as much at fellow Islamics as at American "infidels." Their fierce attacks on the defilement that they believe they see everywhere in contemporary life resemble those of past movements and sects from all parts of the world; such sects, with end-of-the-world prophecies and devout violence in the service of bringing those prophecies about, flourished in Europe from the eleventh through the sixteenth century. Similar sects like the fanatical Japanese cult Aum Shinrikyo, which released sarin gas into the Tokyo subways in 1995, have existed—even proliferated—in our own time.

The American apocalyptic entity is less familiar to us. Even if its urges to power and domination seem historically recognizable, it nonetheless represents a new constellation of forces bound up with what I've come to think of as "superpower syndrome." By that term I mean a national mindset—put forward strongly by a tight-knit leadership group—that takes on a sense of omnipotence, of unique standing in the world that grants it the right to hold sway over all other nations. The American superpower status derives from our emergence from World War II as uniquely powerful in every respect, still more so as the only superpower left standing at the end of the Cold War in the early 1990s.

More than merely dominate, the American superpower now seeks to control history. Such cosmic ambition is accompanied by an equally vast sense of entitlement, of special dispensation to pursue its aims. That entitlement stems partly from historic claims to special democratic virtue, but has much to do with an embrace of technological power translated into military terms. That is, a superpower—the world's only superpower—is entitled to dominate and control precisely because it is a superpower.

The murderous events of 9/11 hardened that sense of entitlement as nothing else could have. Superpower syndrome did not require 9/11, but the attacks on the Twin Towers and the Pentagon rendered us an *aggrieved superpower*, a giant violated and made vulnerable, which no superpower can permit. Indeed, at the core of superpower syndrome lies a powerful fear of vulnerability. A superpower's victimization brings on both a sense of humiliation and an angry determination to restore, or even

3

extend, the boundaries of a superpower-dominated world. Integral to superpower syndrome are its menacing nuclear stockpiles and their world-destroying capacity.

Throughout the decades of the Cold War, the United States and the Soviet Union both lived with a godlike nuclear capacity to obliterate the cosmos, along with a fear of being annihilated by the enemy power. Now America alone possesses that world-destroying capacity, and post-Soviet Russia no longer looms as a nuclear or superpower adversary. We have yet to grasp the full impact of this exclusive capacity to blow up anyone or everything, but its reverberations are never absent in any part of the world.

The confrontation between Islamist and American versions of planetary excess has unfortunately tended to define a world in which the vast majority of people embrace neither. But apocalyptic excess needs no majority to dominate a landscape. All the more so when, in their mutual zealotry, Islamist and American leaders seem to act in concert. That is, each, in its excess, nurtures the apocalypticism of the other, resulting in a malignant synergy.

As a psychiatrist concerned with history, I have in my past work explored the destructive excesses of our times—Nazi genocide, the atomic bombings of Hiroshima and Nagasaki, Chinese Communist "thought reform," the Vietnam war, and the apocalyptic forays of Aum Shinrikyo and other cults of the late-twentieth century. Each of these expressed a powerful impulse to destroy the existing world so that it might be purified and renewed. The Nazis had a vision of renewing the world biologically by ridding it of "defiling" races and bad genes. In dropping atomic bombs on two Japanese cities, the United States sought not only to end a bloody war but also to display its awesome power and so to alter and reshape the postwar world to come. Chinese thought reform aimed at rooting out bad thoughts and ill-formed minds associated with an old and corrupt regime and way of life in order to purify, politically and ethically, a vast society. In Vietnam, villages, towns, and parts of cities had to be sacrificed and so destroyed in order to be "saved" from Communism. And Shoko Asahara, the guru who formed the Aum Shinrikyo cult, dedicated it to achieving a biblical Armageddon in order to bring on a world of spiritual perfection.

These extreme twentieth-century dreams and expressions of totalistic control and mass killing were bound to reverberate in the twenty-first century. On September 11, 2001, some of those reverberations became all too cruelly evident. My past work suddenly became current. Indeed, my last book of the twentieth century had been entitled *Destroying the World to Save It*.

PSYCHOLOGY AND HISTORY

The "psychohistorical approach" I have used in all of my studies is no more than the application of psychological methods to historical questions. While I have been much influenced by the psychoanalytic tradition, and especially by the work of Erik Erikson, I have found it necessary to modify that tradition considerably in order to address some of the historical convulsions of our time. In the classical Freudian model, our energies are derived from our instincts or "drives," sexual and aggressive, and from the psychological defenses we call forth to cope with these drives, notably repression. But the cataclysmic events I have studied required a different emphasis: a focus on death and the continuity of life, or the symbolization of life and death. That kind of model or "paradigm" is, I believe, appropriate for any study of collective behavior.

To examine people's struggles in the midst of the most extreme upheavals of the last half century has also required me to supplement their ordinary nitty-gritty level of function—their everyday struggles with love, family, work, and overall self-esteem—with a focus on an ultimate level, that of larger human connectedness, or what I call symbolic immortality. Here I mean combining the knowledge that we die with a quest to be part of something larger than the self: a sense of living on in children and grandchildren; in religious expressions of an immortal soul; in one's "works" or influences on other human beings; in what most cultures describe as "eternal nature"; or in experiences of transcendence ("high states" so intense that within them time and death disappear). This quest for symbolic immortality is of great importance for all of us, but becomes particularly crucial for grasping the experience of people undergoing historical convulsions.

I have done most of my work through direct interviews, face-to-face encounters with twentieth-century victims and victimizers: with death-haunted Hiroshima survivors, with Nazi doctors who participated in medical killing and with their victims who survived the death camps, with Chinese and Westerners subjected to "thought reform," with American Vietnam veterans who turned against their own war but had difficulty extricating themselves from it, and with former members of the Aum Shinrikyo cult still longing for their lost guru. I sought out these people because they had in important ways acted upon or themselves been acted upon by history. Throughout I have looked for what I call "shared themes" in such people in order to shed light not only on their own experience but on that of their—and our—larger historical era.

Looking now at the intricate maneuvers taking place between Islamist apocalyptics and our political leaders, I find much that is unnervingly familiar from my past studies. In this book I explore the themes those involved in perpetrating apocalyptic violence share, seeking always to apply what I have learned from past studies of related behavior.

History includes a powerful set of forces that inevitably involve the researcher as well. Yet history is not something just "out there"—somewhere in the larger cosmos—but is part of the inner self of each of us, and of the shared intellectual and emotional life of the groups and movements discussed in this study.

For me, this book is a strange form of homecoming. My previous studies have been of events that occurred in Europe, Japan, China, or Vietnam. Now we are all dealing with issues of terrorism, suffering, and survival in the "homeland," and the deeply problematic responses of that land and its leaders. For America finds itself at the epicenter of apocalyptic contagion, whether as victim or as perpetrator.

9/11 CONTINUES

More than that, 9/11 is not over. We are still in it. While writing this book, I have become aware of the ways in which I, too, am a survivor of 9/11—not in the sense of having been directly victimized by the attacks but because like all Americans, I was exposed to the intense death-related imagery of a suicidal assault on my country. Those televised images had a near-apocalyptic aura for almost everyone. Hence the immediate reference to the space where the two towers collapsed as "Ground Zero," a term previously reserved for the hypocenter of a nuclear explosion. This continuing sense of disaster places me in quite a different relationship to my subject than in my previous studies. True, most of them focused on relatively recent occurrences whose effects were very much still with us. But, Vietnam aside (and in that work I was on another continent, many thousand miles from the war in question), I was looking at them retrospectively. It is impossible as yet to look at 9/11 in retrospect. Its active reverberations are everywhere. We remain in thralldom to what happened on that day. The dynamic of 9/11 dominates American thought and our current national life.

Our invasion of Iraq reflects the web of deception that the Bush administration, through its "war on terrorism," has woven around the events of that September morning. By all objective evidence Iraq had nothing to do with 9/11, but as Secretary of Defense Donald Rumsfeld suggested on the day after the attacks, the broad definition of that "war" would require us to invade Iraq. At that moment, Iraq rose to the surface from the deeper dreams and visions of our leaders—and so the moment became one of opportunity. To facilitate that policy our leaders then either made, or encouraged by innuendo, the false claim that Iraq was indeed implicated in 9/11, and by the time of the invasion about 50 percent of Americans had come to believe that falsehood.

A deception on such a large scale could only occur because Americans remained genuinely fearful of terrorist attacks even more lethal than 9/11, and because that fear, that sense of vulnerability, could be manipulated to support larger and more ambitious policy aims. It became possible to redirect the fear from Osama bin Laden to another hated Middle Eastern figure, Saddam Hussein, to the point where the two became virtually interchangeable. If anything, American fear of another 9/11 has been intensified by the "successful" invasion and so remains available for use in other situations.

September 11 was a triumphant moment for Islamist fanatics—and a profoundly humiliating one for the leaders of the American superpower, who early on decided that their response would be "war" and a specifically American war at that. They then rejected a measured international response to terrorism, offered specifically by the secretary general of the United Nations, a response that would have included the use of force in focused ways short of war, to hunt down the terrorists and bring them to justice, while mobilizing the enormous outpouring of sympathy for our country expressed throughout the world. Instead, this administration chose to respond unilaterally with the rhetoric of war, making it clear that we alone would decide what levels of military force to apply and who to apply it to, accepting no restraints in the process.

In that and other ways we have responded apocalyptically to an apocalyptic challenge. We have embarked on a series of wars—first in Afghanistan, then in Iraq, with suggestions of additional targeted countries in the offing—because we have viewed the amorphous terrorist enemy as evil and dangerous. But our own amorphously extreme response feeds a larger dynamic of apocalyptic violence, even as it constructs a twenty-first-century version of American empire.

That prospective empire is confusing to the world, to Americans, and perhaps even to those who espouse it. It does not follow prior imperial models of keeping an extensive bureaucracy in place in subject countries and thereby ruling territories extending over much of the earth. Instead, we press toward a kind of control from a distance: mobile forays of military subjugation with subsequent governmental arrangements unclear. Crucial to this kind of *fluid world control* is our dominating war machine, backed by no less dominant nuclear stockpiles. Such an arrangement can lend itself to efforts at the remote control of history. Any such project, however, becomes enmeshed in fantasy, in dreams of imposing an omnipotent will on others, and in the urge to control history itself. Driven by superpower syndrome, such visions of domination and control can prove catastrophic when, as they must, they come up against the irredeemable stubbornness of reality.

While this book tells a grim psychological tale, the telling is an expression of hope. The outcome of the tale is not fixed. Diagnosing our ailment can be a step toward its amelioration or possibly even its cure.

CHAPTER 2

APOCALYPTIC VIOLENCE

Think of apocalyptic violence as a form of ultimate idealism, a quest for spiritual utopia. The word *apocalypse* derives from the Greek term for "revelation" or "uncovering." In Judaism and Christianity, the apocalyptic revelation came from God and concerned a powerful event. In Christianity especially, the event came to be understood as the end of the world itself, or as a prophecy of that end. What gives these visions their allure is that such an end, involving untold vistas of destruction, only foretold a new beginning. All-consuming violence in obliterating a hopelessly corrupt world was, in fact, required for the hopeful and lofty rebirth that was to follow.

Apocalyptic imagery exists in all the major religions. Since it is most specifically a part of Jewish and Christian doctrine, students of religion have rightly warned against invoking Western assumptions when interpreting Islam.

But Islam contains its own versions of the apocalyptic, as in fact do secular projections of world destruction and re-creation found in extreme ideological movements like Communism and Fascism. Such imagery is part of a universal mythology of death and rebirth. As the student of world mythology Joseph Campbell put it, "Death-and-rebirth, rebirth through ritual . . . is an extremely ancient [idea] in the history of culture." Spiritual rebirth is a goal so desirable that the annihilation of everything else on its behalf may feel justified. A recent statement by an Islamist zealot offers an indication of how far one might go on behalf of perfect spiritual renewal: "We believe in the principle of establishing *Sharia* [the Islamic moral and criminal code] even if this means the death of all mankind."

THE MCVEIGH APOCALYPSE

Examples of apocalyptic violence are everywhere in the world, though not always recognized as such when they come from our part of it. For instance, we think of Timothy McVeigh as a lone fanatic who in 1995 blew up the Murrah Federal Building in Oklahoma City, killing 168 people, because he was enraged at his government. Such a characterization, however, neglects the apocalyptic dimensions of his act. He felt himself to be one of many believers dedicated to bringing a new world into being. His fervent hope was that in destroying a government building he would set off a chain reaction. Others, inspired by him, would do the same throughout the country, starting a vastly destructive "revolutionary" process that would lead to the rebirth of our country as a purified white Aryan nation.

He saw himself as part of a vast secular crusade that had already begun, for he was devoted to what may be the most apocalyptically murderous volume ever written, a novel by the American neo-Nazi leader William Pierce called *The Turner Diaries*. (Assigning it to students for a class of mine felt like assigning them Hitler's *Mein Kampf* updated with nuclear weapons.) McVeigh carried this novel with him everywhere, gave it to people as a gift, sold it at gun shows, and was said to have slept with it under his pillow. The novel's protagonist, Earl Turner, is part of a successful revolution of "white patriots" against the American government, which has come under the evil influence of Jews and blacks and is taking guns away from whites in order to subject them to defiled races. The revolutionaries not only succeed in taking over the government but then employ nuclear, biological, and chemical weapons to systematically annihilate all Jews and all nonwhites throughout the world.

Turner becomes a great revolutionary "martyr" by crashing a plane armed with a nuclear weapon into the Pentagon, a fantasy of Pierce's that eerily anticipated the 9/11 attack. It has frequently been pointed out that McVeigh found in *The Turner Diaries* instructions for making and using the fertilizer bomb he would employ to such murderous effect in Oklahoma City. More instructive for him, however, was Turner's apocalyptic, if fictional, martyrdom and the novel's overall vision of world destruction in the service of the political/spiritual perfection of a "New Era."

ANTAGONISTS IN THE MIDDLE EAST

Similarly apocalyptic visions underlie much of the terrorism in the Middle East. Palestinian Hamas suicide bombers, for instance, have had an immediate political goal: interrupting any suggestion of the peace process, which they strongly oppose. But the group's larger vision is of a holy war in which the Jews of Israel are the designated victims. Hamas's charter declares that "Allah is [our] goal, the Prophet its model, the Quran its Constitution, jihad its path, and death for the cause of Allah its most sublime belief." It speaks of a world-ending mystical process of purification in which even rocks and trees "will cry O Muslim! There is a Jew hiding behind me, come and kill him!"

Parallel currents run through Israeli terrorism. Yigal Amir, who murdered Prime Minister Yitzhak Rabin on November 4, 1995, was no less intent than any Hamas militant upon interrupting the peace process, though mainly because in his mind it threatened to delay the appearance of the Messiah. He belonged to a version of Jewish messianism in which "the Messiah's coming requires Jewish possession of all biblical lands promised to our ancestors." Amir also did not experience himself as alone. For instance, he held in esteem Dr. Baruch Goldstein, who, in February 1994, walked into a mosque at the Cave of the Patriarchs (a holy site shared by Muslims and Jews) with an automatic weapon and gunned down twenty-nine Palestinians at morning prayer. Like Goldstein (and in a sense like McVeigh), Amir considered himself "an agent of the Redemption," obligated to "change history and return the messianic process to its course." Amir was acting upon a long-antiquated Talmudic precept of *din rodef*—revived by a number of like-minded rabbis—the duty of a Jew to kill another Jew designated as a traitor because he has given away Jewish land or imperiled the lives of Jews.

In Amir's expression of Jewish apocalypticism through assassination, there was a deep conviction that "at the End of Days, the 'believers,' the Sons of Light, will defeat the heretics, the Sons of Darkness." Amir's act was an expression of the biblical politics that energize Jewish extremists, including many in the movement to settle the occupied Palestinian lands on the West Bank.

So we encounter in the Middle East contending forces, each viewing itself as on a sacred mission of murder in order to renew the world. While these apocalyptic groups are not in the majority, they can manage to dominate events by acting more or less in concert, responding to each other's acts with murderous passion, stimulating one another to set a tone of continuous confrontation and killing. In this vicious circle, feelings of grief and loss on both sides are transformed again and again into vengeful rage, which sooner or later take hold in ordinary people not otherwise committed either to holy war or to biblical politics. These feelings are profoundly intensified by the passionate survivor memories of both groups: Jews in connection with the Holocaust, and Palestinians in connection with earlier European imperialism and with more recent losses of land and homes through wars with the Israelis.

This kind of dance of death involving antagonistic apocalyptic groups continues to take place not only in the Middle East but throughout the world, including on the Indian subcontinent, where Hindu and Islamic fundamentalists are "partners" in terror and killing; in the United States; and in other places where Islamist religious zealots and militaristic American anti-terrorist zealots "partner" in their own dance. Such contending groups everywhere almost seem to seek each other out, making use of any ensuing confrontations to reenergize their own apocalyptic impulses. While such interaction has certainly existed in the past, contemporary global information technology enhances and speeds up the process. More than that, the weaponry now exists that could transform the world-destructive dreams of such partners into a dreadful reality. To these jarring facts of our age, I'll soon return.

APOCALYPSE AND HUMAN NATURE

The image of apocalypse has been so much with us because we are meaning-hungry creatures who know that we die, and we fervently seek a place for our deaths in the cosmic order. Individual death, when associated with the death and rebirth of the world, can take on special significance and high nobility. That sequence is ritualized in ceremonies of the New Year, in which (according to historian of religion Mircea Eliade) "the world is destroyed and re-created"—often, in premodern societies, in ways that permit a revival of the dead. Through apocalyptic myths, not just individual but collective life and death becomes bound up with a cosmic process that claims dominion over "the nature and purpose of history."

Participation in an apocalyptic project offers expression for two primal human aspirations—the urge toward spiritual or ethical improvement, in this case through an embrace of what is perceived as radical good; and the urge to become part of something not just larger than oneself but also sacred and eternal. That powerful sense of immortality can be intoxicating, enough to transform one's existence and offer a new perspective on life itself.

"Physical death is not an ultimate disaster" as religious scholar John Collins puts it. "There is a life, and there are values which go beyond, or transcend, death. The purpose of [the] apocalyptic is to foster the cherishing of values which transcend death and thereby the experience of transcendent life."

That sense of a transcendent cosmic order can be internalized and the individual believer is suddenly made to feel his life newly purposeful and in touch with eternity. More than just a sense of immortality, he experiences himself in alliance with the deity—or with history—enabling him to share in His or its ultimate power to destroy and re-create. Feelings of weakness or despair can be replaced by a surge of life-power or even omnipotence.

The theme of the destruction of a corrupt world by a stern deity in order to clear the way for a new spiritual beginning has been so pervasive as to be a common denominator of the world's major religions. Long predating Christianity and Judaism, it can, in fact, be traced back to the Iranian prophet Zoroaster in the fifteenth century B.C. Yet, however ancient it may be, for believers the apocalyptic is experienced as overwhelmingly immediate in its power, and the present is seen as offering "a decisive opportunity for the transformation of the world." In that way a 3,500-year-old vision of destruction and re-creation becomes a fiercely rewarding contemporary expectation of a soon-to-be or a distant but revelatory future.

But whatever the psychological satisfaction obtained, the apocalyptic cannot rest easy. He feels always under pressure to impose his world view—antagonistic to much contemporary rationality—on others, in part to stifle his own doubts and affirm the virtue of his convictions. He is a restless missionary who can become a righteous killer.

What he shares with all of us is the universal impulse to spiritualize death, to find some larger meaning in the continuity of life. That tendency is expressed by most cultures in funeral rituals that de-emphasize the physical evidence of death, the dead body, while embracing and nurturing the immortal soul. Whatever its extremity, the apocalyptic imagination has its beginnings in ordinariness, in the conundrum we human beings experience in the face of death. This is why there is always the potential for a version of the apocalyptic imagination to appear.

FROM TAME TO VIOLENT APOCALYPSE

It is important to remember that historically the apocalyptic imagination has usually been nonviolent in nature. Apocalyptic imagery provided assurance that God was in control of history; that there was a "divinely predetermined pattern of crisis, judgment, and vindication"; that for those patient enough, a time of cleansing and rebirth was on its way. Indeed, such apocalypticism is "the mother of all Christian theology," and apocalyptic visions, Christian or otherwise, have flourished during times of great suffering. They have been powerful sources of hope for relief from pain, for the appearance of God's justice, for evil and suffering to give way to spiritual beauty and perfection.

What psychological steps, then, render the apocalyptic believer violent? First, there is the sense that the life of one's group is profoundly threatened—so much so that the group is inundated with death anxiety. That plight—the death anxiety itself—is attributed to the spread of evil. Since the death anxiety can only be eased by the disappearance of evil and the evil can only be overcome by a realization of the apocalypse, there develops a hungry impatience for its realization. The evil being confronted is viewed as something like an enemy army, which must not only be defeated but, since ever ready to regroup, annihilated. For that task one requires what the writer James Carroll calls "god-sponsored violence"—violence that is both unlimited and holy. As individuals and as a group, then, apocalyptics merge with God in the claim to *ownership of death*. That is, they claim the right not only to murderous purification but to make all judgments concerning who is to die and who is to be permitted to survive. This ownership of death comes to include ownership of meaning and of all aspects of life.

Apocalyptic violence becomes the ultimate form of collective regeneration. We may say that death is totalized, is focused upon as the source of this regeneration and the decisive indicator of apocalyptic achievement. Whether through killing or martyrdom, death becomes equated with immortality. Any such killing or dying is understood as part of God's control over history. In deciding who lives and who dies, zealots are invoking what they claim to be God's project. The principle of death and rebirth becomes rebirth through killing and dying.

GRANDIOSITY AND PARANOIA

The apocalyptic project is nothing if not grandiose. What could be more grandiose than a vast plan to save the world by destroying it while exercising ownership over death itself? But for participants, it is not them but God (or the equivalent) who is being grandiose, and He has full claim to be just that. Simply acting under God's grandiose canopy, a believer's most prosaic everyday struggles can be enlarged and ennobled as part of a glorious and sanctified realm of destruction and redemption.

Leaders and instigators of apocalyptic projects, in their claimed alliance with God (or history), become grandiose and sometimes megalomanic: grandiose in their exaggeration of personal status, and megalomanic in subsuming the world to the self in the name of God, even *replacing* the world with the self. I found these characteristics on florid display in Shoko Asahara, the guru of the Japanese Aum Shinrikyo cult. He claimed to have achieved "the state of a Buddha who has attained mirrorlike wisdom," to be the "divine emperor" of Japan and of the world, "the holiest holy man," and the "last twentieth-century savior." One can also assume grandiosity bordering on megalomania (if sometimes exhibited in less florid form) in others who take the lead in projects of apocalyptic destruction, including not only Osama bin Laden but also (much affected by their unprecedented power) American proponents of world domination and the control of history.

Followers of such zealots, through a process of merging with them, gain ready access to that grandiose realm. They share in the store of godlike and God-dispensed power and righteousness associated with destroying and purifying the world. The very extremity of the project— its brutality and cosmic reach—can create in disciples a powerful sense of more-than-mortal status. In this and other ways, ordinary people can be socialized to what most of us would consider a bizarre mindset of apocalyptic violence and the still more bizarre, even barbaric actions that tend to follow it. Such a participatory disciple is offered precious psychological rewards—repeated experiences of transcendence (what Aum Shinrikyo members called "mystical experiences"), which are bound up with a sense of collective transcendence that pervades the group, and the approval of the guru or leader, perceived as the approval of God or of history itself.

Inseparable from this grandiosity is the paranoid edge of the apocalyptic mindset. Leader and followers feel themselves constantly under attack—threatened not just with harm but with annihilation. For them that would mean the obliteration of everything of value on this degraded planet, of the future itself. They *must* destroy the world in order to survive themselves. This is why they in turn feel impelled to label as absolute evil and annihilate any group that seems to impede their own sacred mission.

Such a sense of paranoid aggressiveness is more readily

detectable in the case of certified zealots like Asahara or bin Laden. But it is by no means absent from the minds of American strategists who, though possessing overwhelming military dominance, express constant fear of national annihilation, and embark upon aggressive or "preemptive" military actions.

To speak of apocalyptic leaders as having a paranoid edge is not to say that they are psychiatrically ill. Some can be, of course, if their paranoia is part of a psychosis (a form of psychological breakdown in which there is a thought disorder and severely impaired social function); and some can move in and out of psychosis. But more often they are not psychotic and can function quite effectively in mobilizing followers for apocalyptic projects. Indeed, paranoid people can frequently function at relatively high intellectual levels. There can be an in-between diagnosis, that of "paranoid personality," essentially describing a person who goes through life with notably paranoid tendencies. (Most of the time Asahara, Aum Shinrikyo's guru, could have been considered a paranoid personality, but under duress he would move into actual psychosis, becoming increasingly removed from reality.) In general, severe paranoia contains strong elements of underlying death anxiety and fear of annihilation, along with rage toward one's alleged attackers. Feeling always vulnerable and besieged, the paranoid person is inclined to strike first.

Followers can be drawn into the guru's or leader's paranoia and thereby find expression for similar tendencies in themselves. What results is a shared state of group paranoia that can be sustained all too effectively and a source of extreme acts that few of the participants would have considered by themselves. In this way a collective grandiosity can take on a dangerous paranoid dimension.

The progression from an apocalyptic vision to acts of apocalyptic violence requires a radical ideology that absorbs and articulates this intense paranoia. While the vision itself polarizes the world into clear categories of good and evil, the killing of those on the evil side of the divide requires the visceral sense of danger that paranoia provides. It is ordinarily not enough for an apocalyptic group simply to imagine itself ridding the world of evil for the sake of a glorious renewal. There must be a more immediate perception of threat related to death and annihilation. Precisely that kind of searing individual and collective death anxiety, together with an equally powerful promise of transcending death via the sacred project, enables participants to take the radical step of killing large numbers of their fellow human beings.

FORCING THE END

The goals of apocalyptic violence can be confusing. Sometimes they may seem specifically political; at other times, wildly amorphous, cosmic, limitless. In fact, apocalyptic movements encompass both dimensions. Aum Shinrikyo, for instance, sought to weaken or destroy its designated enemies—defectors from or critics of the cult, rival religious leaders, and the Japanese authorities. At the same time, by releasing sarin gas in the Tokyo subway system and planning other projects of random mass killing, it was attempting to initiate World War III and bring about a literal biblical Armageddon. Shoko Asahara's aggressive version of what I've called "attack guruism" was in the service of "action prophecy"—that is, of violence intended to make his own prophecies come true.

The ancient Hebrews spoke of similar impulses toward what they called "forcing the end"—engaging in violent actions in order to hasten the appearance of the Messiah, knowing that widespread destruction must precede this yearned-for moment. Gershom Scholem, the distinguished scholar of Jewish mysticism, has spoken of those "who could not wait for the arrival of the Messiah but thought to do something for it themselves." Another scholar has called them "messiah-intoxicated Zealots" who "tried to bring about the final redemption by forcing the hand of God." Rabbis eventually condemned this impatient messianism, insisting that "the Messiah would come only when God decided to send him."

But the phenomenon has hardly disappeared from our world. The hubris of "forcing the end" periodically expresses itself in militant apocalyptic movements. It may be at the heart of any grandiose claim to the ownership of death. All this is part of the universal human struggle with death and the continuity of life. Hence, the grandiose killing project of forcing the end is all too much part of the human psychological repertoire. Throughout most of history, apocalyptic sects rarely have moved from dreaming of or praying for the end of time to forcing that end. Part of the reason was that the human means to force such an end did not seem to be at hand. But in our time, the means to force the end have caught up with apocalyptic dreams. Now those dreams are being married to apocalyptic weaponry (or at least the visions of obtaining it), and the idea of acting immediately to force the end is increasingly taking hold in apocalyptic movements.

A compelling theology—or in secular terms, ideology— with a world-ending narrative has been required to activate this human potential. That theology must forcefully divide the world into good and evil, and prescribe the necessary world destruction and renewal, all the while infusing believers with powerful currents of revitalization. All religions can provide such stories of cosmic redemption, but the Christian Armageddon narrative has had particular appeal—and not just in Christian hands— in its concreteness and simplicity, in its high-action rendering of death-and-rebirth mythology.

Even secular movements like the Nazis have followed a version of the Armageddon script. Hitler's followers sought to destroy much of what they saw as a racially polluted world by means of a vast biological purification program. Despite being murderously anti-Jewish and significantly anti-Christian as well, the Nazis drew upon what was most apocalyptic in both of those traditions. The Nazis came to epitomize the apocalyptic principle of *killing to heal*, of destroying vast numbers of human beings as therapy for the world.

APOCALYPTIC MARTYRDOM

The idea of apocalyptic martyrdom intensifies the ordeal of the killer as well as his claim to spiritual renewal, while dramatizing his death as transcending those of his victims. The martyr brings his own being—the sacrifice of his own life—into the dynamic of world destruction and re-creation, thus exemplifying that death-and-rebirth process. In dying to renew the world, both he and his cause are immortalized. In this way he projects his life and his death into the realm of the transcendent and makes a profoundly desired connection between death and immortality.

No wonder that virtually all religions, while condemning ordinary suicide, extol some version of martyrdom. The word *martyr* stems from the Greek term for witness; the martyr bears witness to evil with his own life. He does so, according to official narratives, willingly. (Closer study sometimes reveals ambivalence or reluctant submission on the part of the martyr, and considerable psychological pressure can be exerted in the process of socializing people to martyrdom.) The historical examples most frequently called forth all emphasize that such sacrificial witness becomes part of the death and rebirth of one's own people: Jewish martyrs before a Roman legion at Masada; Christian martyrs among various "heathens," notably during the Crusades; and Islamic martyrs among "infidels" and "apostates," past and present. In such cases, the martyr's suffering and dying are often connected with killing. With apocalyptic martyrdom in particular, the individual's death is likely to be subsumed to a massive killing project.

At times killers are designated as martyrs not because they must die but because they must call forth superhuman powers to steel themselves for their "ordeal" in killing large numbers of other human beings. That was the case with the Nazis when Heinrich Himmler, the regime's leading planner of mass murder, praised his SS troops for their personal "sacrifice" in carrying out the difficult task of shooting vast numbers of Jews face-to-face. He spoke of the profound difficulty of the killers' task in seeing before them "a hundred corpses . . . side by side, or five hundred, or a thousand" and of the "heroism" involved in carrying out the killings. Himmler made clear to the killers that their actions on behalf of an ennobling project of racial purification would remain a proud secret, "an unwritten and never-to-be-written page of glory."

In contrast, the al–Qaeda hijackers of September 11, 2001, were part of a martyrdom project that was meant to be visibly, globally apocalyptic. It was to be broadcast worldwide to the greater glory of their purifying cause. Yet they, too, were carefully prepared by their leader, Mohammad Atta, for their "ordeal" to come. They were given detailed instructions for carrying out their task—what to wear, how to behave, how to focus their minds, how to invoke Allah—which were the final steps in socializing the hijackers to their martyrdom and also an expression of pragmatic recognition that there was indeed an ordeal involved. In both the Nazi and al–Qaeda cases, the participants in mass killing were encouraged to focus on the transcendent cause they were serving. While in one case the protagonists gave their lives and in the other they simply gunned people down, for both groups martyrdom resided in the sacrificial ordeal of carrying out a murderous project.

Nor is this kind of martyrdom absent from the American imagination. We do not know exactly how Timothy McVeigh steeled himself for his act, but we do know how *The Turner Diaries* author William Pierce imagined his novel's hero doing so before initiating his nuclear attack on the Pentagon. Just a few days earlier, Pierce has Turner declare to members of the mystical revolutionary Order, "Brothers! . . . I offer you my life," and they reply in chorus: "Brother! We accept your life. In return we offer you everlasting life in us. Your deed shall not . . . be forgotten, until the end of time."

Turner records in his diary his joy at the prospect of martyrdom: "What I will do today will be of more weight in the annals of the race than all the conquests of Caesar and Napoleon—if I succeed!" He then makes careful arrangements before his final mission for his diary to be preserved, so that it can "outlive . . . me," an arrangement "we owe to our dead, to our [previous] martyrs: that we do not forget them or their deeds." Though originally suggested as an act of penance (for having revealed, under torture, the names of fellow revolutionaries), Turner's martyrdom becomes one of absolute and self-conscious glory in serving his apocalyptic cause.

CONSUMED BY FIRE

Apocalyptic destruction is invariably imagined as devouring flames. The "fire and brimstone" and "lake of fire" of the Book of Revelation extend to such twentieth-century events as the Nazi crematoria, the firestorms of the World War II bombings of Dresden and Tokyo, the atomic firestorms of Hiroshima and Nagasaki, and the twenty-first-century gasoline-fueled fires of the Twin Towers. This idea of flames as the ultimate form of annihilation has long been ritualized in one of the most terrible of all individual religious punishments, "burning at the stake." Evil must be totally "consumed"—actively and painfully destroyed, reduced to ashes, to nothingness—before the world can be truly renewed. Inevitably, the flames of the Book of Revelation and those of nuclear devastation have, for large numbers of people, converged.

Yet a very different image of world destruction that includes neither fire nor promise of renewal entered the world in the mid-twentieth century. I have in mind the global nuclear desolation frequently imagined over the course of the Cold War and given macabre expression by Nevil Shute in his 1957 novel *On the Beach*. Shute depicts a post-nuclear world in which the few who remain alive quietly await their deaths from radiation fallout. Similar scenes of eerie nuclear wastelands were associated with the neutron bomb, thought to destroy all human life while leaving intact the world's buildings, towns, and cities. In these images, silent and invisible contamination replaces all-consuming biblical fire. Such scenes were meant to suggest the end of the human world with no possibility of renewal. But present-day apocalyptic thought has seized upon precisely this sort of desolation as a possible means of fulfillment, and has made it a part of contemporary narratives of cosmic death and rebirth.

CHAPTER 3
CENTURY OF EXCESS

No one doubts that we live in the wake of twentieth-century excess. What we can see now is the apocalyptic nature of that excess and how closely it was related to various malignant claims to the ownership of death. Looking at World War I and the Armenian genocide, World War II and the Holocaust, Soviet and Chinese Communism, the atomic bombings of Hiroshima and Nagasaki, the Vietnam war, genocides in Cambodia and Rwanda, and near-genocidal acts and wars in the former Yugoslavia, we can say that the last century was an arena of contending visions of purification, one seemingly more murderous than the next. I have studied a number of these events, in each of which the killing was part of a terrible illusion of rejuvenation.

THE NAZI LEGACY
The Nazis epitomized apocalyptic killing in the twentieth

century. To be sure, Nazi behavior was profoundly influenced by two extreme events earlier in the century: the killing fields of World War I that led to a disastrous German defeat, in Nazi eyes due to a "stab in the back" by those at home who desecrated the glorious sacrifices of the German soldiers in the war; and the Turkish genocide of more than one million Armenians in 1915 under cover of that war (which Hitler considered sufficiently forgotten a couple of decades later for him to feel confident that he could carry out his own genocidal plans against the Jews without future reprisal). Nor, it turns out, were the Nazis even the greatest killers of the century. The Russian Communists and the Chinese Communists each killed more people than did the Nazis. The Nazis were unique, however, in their systematic focus on a comprehensive genocidal project that was a specific expression of an elaborate, totalistic ideology. The regime's apocalyptic mindset was exhibited in the priority Hitler and much of the SS gave to killing Jews, even when the war effort took second place as a result. The most extreme form of the Nazi apocalyptic mindset resided in those SS mystical theorists who insisted that, should every last Jew in the world be killed, a form of universal utopia would ensue.

The Nazis' biological focus enabled them to medicalize their apocalypse. Their ideology emphasized "curing" the Nordic race of a deadly Jewish "infection," and Nazi doctors took a leading role in the killing process itself. They made cursory "selections," for instance, at the ramp of the Birkenau/Auschwitz death camp as Jews rounded up all over Europe descended from trains. A small number of Jews, considered strong enough to be admitted to the camp for slave labor, were chosen to live for a while; the rest were sent immediately to their deaths. The doctors then supervised the actual killings in the gas chambers. Moreover, most Nazi death camps evolved from killing centers that had been part of an earlier "euthanasia" program for those loosely judged to have incurable illnesses or genetic defects. All this was part of Nazi *apocalyptic biology*, a vision of ridding the world of "bad genes." More than any other movement, and on many levels, the Nazi regime's signature was its biomedical reversal of healing and killing, so that its deepest principle became that of *killing to heal*.

The Nazis also stimulated apocalyptic tendencies in others. One such example was the Allies' World War II policy of "strategic" or "area" bombing: the leveling of first German and then Japanese cities in attacks specifically aimed at civilian populations. This American and British policy was by no means simply an imitation of Nazi tactics, as is sometimes claimed. The Nazis had indeed bombed civilians in Guernica, Warsaw, Rotterdam, London, and Coventry, but these attacks were on a more limited scale. The British and American military had prepared well prior to World War II to wage an air war specifically aimed at "the enemy civil population, and, in particular . . . the industrial workers." But the British, in initiating the bombings, and the Americans in later joining and expanding them, justified the enterprise with the sense that they were combating an unparalleled evil. In that way, Nazi war-making and mass killing brought about a response that was itself violent in the extreme and a form of global salvation through the flames of destruction.

Americans offered a similar justification for the even more extreme devastation caused by their policy of "saturation bombing"—the massive, carefully planned fire-bombings of virtually all of Japan's highly flammable cities. By that time, a military strategy of attacks on civilian populations had become almost routine. To be sure, civilians had been targeted in modern warfare since at least the time of the American Civil War, but the firestorms that engulfed cities like Dresden and Tokyo and killed many of thousands of civilians in single days could be said to have rendered such policies apocalyptic. The Tokyo raid on the night of 9/10 killed more people, at least initially, than the atomic bombings of either Hiroshima or Nagasaki. Leon Blum, the French Socialist leader, once said that he was certain the Allies would triumph over the Nazis but feared that, in doing so, we would become like them. The sad truth is that in the realm of strategic bombing we went further than they did. We were all too susceptible to escalating twentieth-century technological slaughter in the name of world redemption.

At issue also was a form of apocalyptic contagion. More than a matter of mere technology, we were drawn into the murderous apocalyptic energies of the time. The Nazis did much to unleash these energies, but once we began to express them our own destructive power soon became second to none. Our sense of the evil we encountered was so extreme that we could all too readily do *anything*, including annihilate all of a nation's major cities and kill hundreds of thousands of people, to combat it and bring about historical renewal.

Such apocalyptic contagion is all too evident in our present confrontation with Islamists: in response to one's enemy's pursuit of absolute purification, one seeks to purify absolutely in turn; in the name of destroying evil, each side seeks to destroy not only the other but enough of the world to achieve mystical rebirth.

HIROSHIMA AND GOD'S PURPOSE

Apocalyptic air warfare in World War II culminated in the use of atomic bombs on Hiroshima and Nagasaki. The policy of saturation bombing had been so established that it could readily encompass even what was known to be (if not fully understood as) a revolutionary new weapon. In this way our use of the weapon derived from our struggle against Nazi evil. Indeed, the impetus for embarking on the atomic bomb project—for mobilizing vast economic and scientific resources, including a distinguished group of émigré physicists—came from the all-too-plausible fear that German scientists, much more advanced in nuclear physics than we were, would produce the weapon first for the Nazis, who would then use it against us. Significantly, though, once we had the weapon, our leaders decided to make use of it months after the Germans had surrendered, after the Nazis were no more, and after we knew that they had not been able to produce the atomic bomb in any case—and then, of course, we dropped two of them on a different enemy.

Given the extreme racial antagonisms Americans and Japanese felt and expressed toward one another during World War II, we may assume that it was easier to use the weapon on a nonwhite people than it would have been on Europeans. But considering what we had already done to Europeans in our saturation bombing campaign, along with our unlimited sense of entitlement in pursuing our struggle against evil, I do not doubt that we would have been capable of employing atomic weapons on the Germans as well.

Most historians, pointing to Japan's desperate state in early August 1945 and its series of surrender overtures, have concluded that use of the bomb was in no sense necessary. There were many factors that nonetheless went into the decision to use it—including technological and bureaucratic momentum, domestic political considerations, the doctrine of unconditional surrender we had proclaimed, and the possibility that we would be combating the Soviet Union, our then-ally, in a postwar world. But from the beginning the stated American reason, which certainly had its importance for decision-makers, was that of ending the war quickly and of "saving lives."

That view of the bomb as life-enhancing, which has continued to this day, was an early manifestation of what I call *nuclearism*: the embrace of the weapon as a source not only of transcendent power but of life-sustaining security and peace, and in some cases as close to a deity. Elements of nuclearism could be observed in a few American leaders, in their anticipation of its power for good—before the weapon actually appeared. Even such humane scientists as Leo Szilard and Niels Bohr, who were to become inspiring antinuclear advocates, at first favored dropping the weapon on a human population because they believed the effects would be so impressive that nations would no longer go to war. The bomb's very destructiveness was seen as potentially world-saving as well as world-destroying. Or to put the matter another way, the bomb was to save the world from itself.

Atrocity-producing situations—and anything involving nuclear weapons qualifies as such—take on many forms, but in all of them there is a collective psychological momentum, a shared psychological energy pressing toward cruelty and killing. The most terrible example of this was the experience of Vice President Harry Truman. On April

12, 1945, when Franklin Delano Roosevelt died, he became president and suddenly found himself facing a decision about using a new weapon of unprecedented destructive power of which he had known nothing. Truman stepped into an already existing nuclear environment, dominated by procedures and mindsets strongly pressing toward the bomb's use. Only exceptional people can resist atrocity-producing situations. There has been speculation about whether even Roosevelt, had he been alive, would have had sufficient strength and wisdom to call forth such resistance. It would have required an ethical and historical imagination capable of transcending the intense pressures of the immediate wartime atmosphere, a capacity to extricate oneself from the shared embrace of a new dimension of power in the struggle against evil. In the case of Truman, detailed records suggest that he never permitted himself to imagine a possible alternative to the bomb's use.

It is fair to say that simply building and possessing nuclear weapons creates the potential for an atrocity-producing situation: any assumption of a dangerous threat to American security could initiate a strong technological and psychological momentum toward use. This is likely to be true of any nuclear-weapons–possessing nation or group, and one can never assume that a wise statesman will appear to prevent an apocalyptic act. For nuclear weapons are inherently apocalyptic, and with them America took over a form of the ownership of death, believing it could now be operated in the service of good. That ownership was demonstrated, awesomely and tragically, in Hiroshima and Nagasaki, by means of a revolutionary equation: one plane, one bomb, one city. This was an apotheosis of apocalyptic warfare.

Certainly people in Hiroshima experienced a sense that the whole world was dying. When in 1962 I studied the psychological experiences of the survivors of that still almost unimaginable event, a Japanese physicist described the moment to me in this way: "Everything seemed dark, dark all over. Then I thought, the world is ending." And a Protestant minister remembered: "I thought this was the end of Hiroshima, of Japan, of humankind. This was God's judgment on man." For a woman writer it was "the collapse of the earth which it was said would take place at the end of the world, and which I had read about as a child." And a history professor described to me how, from a hill overlooking the city, "I looked down [and] saw that Hiroshima had disappeared . . . What I felt . . . I just can't explain with words . . . Hiroshima just didn't exist." Even in the absence of Hiroshima's sea of death, American scientists and military officers witnessing the first bomb test in the New Mexico desert described remarkably similar reactions. Brigadier General Thomas Farrell, in his official report, spoke of the "searing light" and "awesome roar" which "warned of doomsday and made us feel that we puny things were blasphemous to dare tamper with the forces heretofore reserved to the Almighty."

Now, for the first time it seemed, the power that had once only been imagined as God's was put into human hands. In apocalyptic visions of the past there had been the assumption that it was *God* who was witnessing the increasing defilement of the world, *His* patience that was exhausted, *He* who decided to invoke *His* power over death and destroy the world and all of its people, in order to re-create it in *His* image. With nuclear weapons, we human beings staked our claim to that godlike prerogative. Such power both deeply attracts us and, not surprisingly, leaves us profoundly uncomfortable.

We have the need, so to speak, to return the power to God. So we readily assume that our own new, godlike capacity, lodged in the weapons, is an aspect of God's will. If, formerly, only God could do it, and now we too can do it, have already done it, and are prepared under the right circumstances to do it again, then God must want us to do it. The inherently apocalyptic dimension of these weapons causes us to associate them with a deified purpose, whether we directly enunciate it or not. In using the bombs on Hiroshima and Nagasaki, therefore, we could view ourselves as carrying out God's purpose of defeating evil.

But we are not fully convinced. America's unease or "raw nerve" in connection with the atomic bombings of those two Japanese cities is reflected in our deep resistance to exploring the full human truths of those bombings. (The cancellation amid much controversy in 1995 of an exhibition seeking to probe the broad Japanese and American experiences of Hiroshima and Nagasaki at the Smithsonian National Air and Space Museum was evidence of how raw this nerve remained half a century later.) There has, in fact, been worldwide resistance to these truths, so much so that my first shock in arriving in Hiroshima in 1962—one could say my first research finding—was the discovery that, seventeen years after an event that was surely one of the tragic turning points in human history, no one had studied its human impact.

Terrorists who might acquire and use nuclear weapons—Aum Shinrikyo sought them, and al–Qaeda has expressed great interest in them—might have far less worry about usurping godlike powers because they already see themselves in all they do as mere agents of the deity. We cannot be sure that such an assumption is absent from the minds of certain American leaders as well. Both Islamist and American zealots, should they participate in an Armageddon-like nuclear sequence, would be combining the inherent apocalyptic dimensions of the weapons with their own apocalyptic ideologies.

The physical capacity for *infinite* killing (literally destroying the world) had to await the hydrogen bomb, first tested in 1952. But that capacity was imaginatively established by the atomic bombings, and not just in the minds of survivors or of witnesses to the first test. The bombings of Hiroshima and Nagasaki were perceived throughout the world as rehearsals for infinite destruction, and in that sense, of man's transgression into the realm of godly power—and various world-ending fantasies and fictions quickly filled the media and entered the movie theaters as well. Imagery of exploding planets has become commonplace in our lives and even in children's cartoons.

In general, nuclear weapons have come to suggest a new dimension of the ownership of death: nothing less than ownership of the death of the world.

VIETNAM—DESTROYING TO SAVE

The apocalyptic aura of the American war in Vietnam was expressed in the classic statement of a soldier, "We had to destroy it [the village] to save it." One could well extend that image to say that much of Vietnam was devastated so that it could be "saved" from Communism. From that standpoint, Vietnam was part of a global mission of purification, meant to combat the defilement and spread of Communist evil.

A mission of that kind readily created what I came to call an "atrocity-producing situation"—a setting in which ordinary soldiers, men no better or worse than you or me, could readily commit atrocities: shooting prisoners, randomly killing civilians, mutilating corpses. That, of course, can happen in any war, but the Vietnam environment, psychologically and structurally, was particularly conducive to atrocity: counterinsurgency warfare in unfamiliar physical and cultural terrain; an enemy with support from the people (whether in common cause or out of fear) who could strike and kill but was hard to directly engage; fighting in which civilians were often impossible to tell apart from military enemies; the "body count" of enemy dead as virtually the only measure of success; "free-fire zones" in which one was permitted to fire virtually at random; and encouragement from officers to avenge the deaths of buddies and to deal with feelings of angry mourning by killing anyone or anything in sight. Contributing to this socialization to atrocity was a mixture of military frustration and radical disbelief in the assigned mission. One former grunt described such feelings to me this way: "What am I doing here? We don't take any land. We don't give it back. We just mutilate bodies. What the fuck are we doing here?"

Like Harry Truman facing his nuclear choice in 1945, most American soldiers sent into battle in Vietnam in those war years of the late 1960s found themselves thrown into an atrocity-producing situation for which they were utterly unprepared. But what I also learned from Vietnam veterans—in the early 1970s I participated in psychologically intense "rap groups" with many who had turned against the war and wished to examine their behavior in fighting it—was that people need not be psychologically stuck forever in such moments. Men and women could experience what I came to think of as "animating guilt" and use it as a means of rejecting the overall American mission in Vietnam and their own part in it. They could express painful forms of self-condemnation without remaining fixed in a static, *mea culpa* stance. Rather, they were capable of leaving both the atrocity-producing situation and the overall apocalyptic mission by transforming those guilt feelings into a sense of responsibility in opposing the war and revealing its grotesque details to the American people—all the while insisting that our leaders and our society acknowledge responsibility for what was being done in our name thousands of miles away.

More recently, Israeli soldiers, sometimes citing the American experience in Vietnam as a model, have similarly come to oppose their war, their country's occupation of Palestinian lands and its army's brutal treatment of Palestinians, by refusing to fight in the occupied territories. Calling their group Courage to Refuse, they declare: "We shall not continue to fight beyond the 1967 borders in order to dominate, expel, starve, and humiliate an entire people." They too have demonstrated an impressive capacity to transform guilt feelings into expressions of responsibility in seeking to redirect their society toward a more humane path.

Both groups had to overcome the psychic numbing associated with their countries' impulses toward violent purification and allow previously suppressed compassionate feelings to surface. A further interesting parallel to these two situations can be found in the animating guilt of people who were involved in the making of, or strategic planning for, atomic and hydrogen bombs and were later able to become powerful and knowledgeable voices warning the world about nuclear dangers.

VIETNAM AND THE SUPERPOWER PSYCHE

Vietnam has special importance for the superpower syndrome as it was the first significant defeat of a superpower in our times. (The earlier Korean War had been a superpower standoff.) Only a little more than a decade later, the lesser superpower, the USSR, was similarly defeated in Afghanistan and soon after suffered a complete imperial collapse and ceased to exist. The Vietnam war demonstrated that a relatively small and technologically limited country could, on its own terrain, win a victory over a superpower— unless that superpower were willing to use weapons of mass destruction and annihilate the smaller country completely. It was evidence, clear enough to those willing to see, that while either superpower was then capable of destroying the world, neither could control the world.

But that hardly meant such aspirations were at an end. President Richard Nixon had spoken bitterly of America as "a pitiful, helpless giant" because of its reluctance to take aggressive military stances in the world that might lead to other Vietnams, a reluctance that came to be known as the "Vietnam syndrome." In the eyes of superpower advocates, that syndrome stood for a form of weakness that had to be overcome. The most ringing words of

President George Bush Sr., in his immediate response to victory in the first Gulf War in 1991, invoked not heroic warriors (as in Winston Churchill's classic "Never have so many owed so much to so few") but a cure: "By God, we've kicked the Vietnam syndrome once and for all!"

For many American planners, even that victory proved insufficient for kicking the syndrome. As an antidote to memories of Vietnam-era "weakness," they constructed military policies of "preemptive" (or preventive) strikes and world hegemony, first resisted by the mainstream but enthusiastically embraced by the second Bush administration after 9/11. Those post-Vietnam policies eventually brought about the invasion of Iraq in April 2003. Rather than accept the truth of superpower limitation that lay beneath the "Vietnam syndrome," such global planners embraced an illusory claim of superpower omnipotence.

THOUGHT REFORM—ENGINEERING THE SOUL

So far, in reviewing the last half-century or more of violent excesses, I have considered purifying impulses, apocalyptic weaponry, and atrocity-producing situations, all with a claim to the ownership of death and through it an imagined rebirth. But a striking aspect of the last century's excesses of particular importance for modern apocalyptic movements has been the assault on the mind. Efforts at manipulation of the mind have been sensationalized in the media as "brainwashing," an arcane, all-powerful process that supposedly no one can resist. (It had perhaps its most famous, if somewhat tongue-in-cheek, expression in the film *The Manchurian Candidate*.) At other times, brainwashing has been nothing more than an epithet for any kind of persuasion of which someone disapproves. In fact, the systematic application of coercive psychological methods for controlling the mind, though certainly echoing earlier historical impulses, has been a crucial twentieth-century phenomenon.

Nowhere has such a project been attempted so deliberately and comprehensively as in Communist China, where approximately one-quarter of the world's population has been subjected to some version of what the Chinese call "thought reform." The process combines two elements: the *confession*, or continuous reiteration of past and present evil acts and thoughts (under considerable psychological and sometimes physical duress); and *reeducation*, the remaking of a person in the reformer's image through pressured and orchestrated criticism and self-criticism. The project's visionary goal was to replace a mental and material past considered thoroughly tainted with a future of perfection of mind and body, and so of the mind and body politic as well. The apocalyptic aim of the process has been nothing less than the ownership of truth and reality—that is, *the ownership of the mind.*

My earliest study of survivors of extreme situations of the previous century involved Chinese and Westerners who had experienced Chinese Communist thought reform. While they varied enormously in their responses, all showed the effects of having been put through a profound ordeal that had threatened or altered their sense of self and world, of personal and collective identity. At certain times in that regime's history (the extraordinary wave of thought reform in 1949–50 and the Great Proletarian Cultural Revolution of 1966–69), the world's most populous nation came to resemble a vast totalistic cult. Most striking about the process was the inability of China's leaders to stop or shut down the urge to control and reform the mind once that urge had been set loose on society.

The Communists arrived as seemingly incorruptible heroes, having undergone legendary ordeals like the epic Long March of 1934–35, a 6,000-mile trek during which more than 80 percent of the original group perished in order to ensure the survival and eventual triumph of the revolution against overwhelming odds. Hence, young Chinese in particular, but many older ones as well, initially responded enthusiastically to the demands of the thought-reform project. It seemed part of the larger project of the rebirth of their country as a strong, independent, revolutionary land after a century of humiliation, collapse, foreign control, and civil war. But even when slowing the project down would have been in the Communists' interest, they were too much in the grip of the impulse toward apocalyptic cleansing to be able to do that. Instead, they overreformed their population, and the repeated waves of confession and reeducation contributed to a widespread sense of suffocation and political alienation.

Originally, Chinese revolutionary leaders viewed thought reform as an alternative to the killing of enemies or dissidents. One of its earliest applications was to captured soldiers of the opposing Nationalist regime during the civil war. Instead of either being put to death or released (to return to the other side or to their homes), they were to be converted and recruited to the Communist army. When the Communists took power, the idea was to enlist the energies of the members of the former regime, as well as of people insufficiently enthusiastic about the new one, and so avoid the Soviet Union's policy of widespread executions of people in those categories. Ironically, once seized by the process of cleansing and recleansing the minds of China, the Communists ended up killing tens of millions of people, killings on a scale at least equaling that of the Soviets. And most of these deaths could be attributed to the very ideological fanaticism or *totalism* that fueled the overall thought-reform project. Such an all-or-none system of belief and morality inexorably carried its practitioners toward what can be called the *dispensing of existence*, the arrogating to themselves of the right to decide who deserves to live and who does not.

The killing that results from such totalism can also be more indirect. That was the case with a national campaign of 1958 hailed as the Great Leap Forward, in which wildly intense thought-reform programs pressed the Chinese population toward creating handmade "backyard furnaces" as substitutes for larger steel factories in bringing rapid industrialization to the country's rural areas. The combination of *psychism* (exaggerated reliance upon will and psychic power to achieve technological or economic goals), and revolutionary enthusiasm (whether or not under duress), caused as many as ninety million people (about a quarter of the active population) to abandon ordinary pursuits and plunge into the illusory "Leap Forward." The result was an extreme shortage of agricultural labor, which, together with false reports of farming efficiency and a drought, led to one of the greatest famines in human history. At least twenty million people—some say as many as forty or even sixty million— starved to death largely because of the apocalyptic ideological fantasies of Mao Zedong, the legendary revolutionary leader who was already in the process of becoming a corrupt potentate.*

Not only did the furnaces "dissolve into piles of mud and bricks after a few rains" but, despite the economic chaos, consistently false reports of success kept coming in

---

*The Cultural Revolution of the late 1960s and early 1970s, which Mao also unleashed, represented an even greater wave of apocalyptic sentiment. But I have focused on the Great Leap Forward as an illustration of the kind of mass dying that can result from indirect apocalyptic violence.

from Communist Party cadres. They were responding to Mao's insistence that ideological purity and revolutionary enthusiasm were always decisive and took precedence over any other kind of economic planning, and as it turned out, over truth itself.

Mao himself was the epicenter of this cataclysmic dying. While this was all happening, he returned to a theme he had initiated two years earlier: the Chinese people, he declared, were "poor and blank," a great advantage because "a clean sheet of paper has no blotches, and so the newest and most beautiful words can be written on it, the newest and most beautiful pictures can be painted on it." At about the same time, in relation to the nuclear confrontation between the Soviet Union and the United States, he speculated that, at worst, perhaps one-half of the 2.7 billion people in the world would die in a nuclear war, but positive developments would follow because "there would still be one-half left; imperialism would be razed to the ground and the whole world would become socialist. After a number of years, the world's population would once again reach 2.7 billion and certainly become even bigger." (One is reminded of parallel projections by American Cold War nuclear strategists like Herman Kahn, celebrating the postnuclear survival of a significant number of [capitalist?] Americans to perpetuate the human race.)

These quotations illustrate the apocalyptic reach of Maoist ideology: the first expresses a view of the mind as infinitely controllable, or, I would say, ownable. The second, equally fantastic, suggests that the killing of more than 1.3 billion people would serve the noble purpose of world renewal. Mao's behavior at that moment—he was then in his mid-sixties and ruling the country from the old Forbidden City in Beijing as a new emperor—suggests to us how an intense apocalyptic immersion transforms a charismatic revolutionary leader into a megalomanic despot and mass murderer. His and his revolution's *quest for ownership of the mind came to be inseparable from the ownership of death*.

These and other examples of twentieth-century excess blend into the larger atmospherics of our era. They contribute to a psychological constellation, a field of energy, that interacts with nonviolent beliefs in apocalypse—the tame apocalypse mentioned earlier—in ways that can carry apocalyptics ever more easily over the threshold into violence. Those images of a tame apocalypse, of world purification and renewal without killing, are always with us, always available for the dangerous transformation into violence. Part of the crossing of that threshold has to do with a group's surge of ideological energy, its turning in on itself sufficiently to overcome all restraints in forcing an end that now seems immediate, concrete, in every sense real. What had been a far-off vision becomes an activist military project of world destruction and rebirth. God is still very much involved, but everything is no longer left to Him.

CHAPTER 4
AUM SHINRIKYO—
THE THRESHOLD CROSSED

um Shinrikyo crossed that threshold of violence with five years still remaining in the twentieth century. Though a relatively small cultic group, it acted upon a vision of cosmic purification that included the murder of just about everyone on earth.

Aum and its guru, Shoko Asahara, burst into world consciousness when the cult released sarin gas in a number of Tokyo subway trains on March 20, 1995. Though tens of thousands of passengers might have been threatened with death, the attack was hurried and inefficient, killing just twelve people, because the group had received word that the police were closing in on them. The group's plan had been to release enormous amounts of sarin later that year in order to create a major disaster and set in motion a series of catastrophic events and so fulfill its guru's world-ending prophecies. According to the plan, Japanese authorities would believe that America had released the sarin; the Americans would assume that the Japanese had done it; a war would break out between the two countries and other great powers would join in, leading to World War III, which would then bring about a biblical Armageddon.

ULTIMATE WEAPONS AND ULTIMATE ZEALOTRY

Now of course that was wild fantasy, but fantasy combined with all-too-real weapons of mass destruction. Aum had produced considerable amounts of sarin, a highly lethal nerve gas (though the guru ordered much of the cult's stockpile destroyed when he became fearful of discovery), and had released various amounts of it on several occasions prior to the Tokyo subway attack. In addition, it had produced biological weapons, notably botulinus and anthrax, and made several unsuccessful attempts to create disasters with them in major urban areas by means of spraying devices. And Aum pursued any avenues it could find for obtaining nuclear weapons. It looked into uranium deposits (even acquiring a ranch in an area of Australia thought to be rich in such deposits), and sought contacts with disaffected Russian nuclear scientists. Particularly active in Russia, Aum made use of its huge financial resources to purchase various kinds of weapons and to bribe officials with access to more of them. Hence the provocative question found in the Russian diary of Aum's leading weapons procurer: "How much does a nuclear warhead cost?"

In the end Aum could not acquire those warheads, and instead made sarin gas its signature weapon. Asahara was fascinated by weapons of mass destruction in general, but sarin might have had a special attraction for him as he greatly admired Hitler and expressed delight when told that the Fuhrer's horoscope closely resembled his own. Sarin had first been produced (though not used) by Hitler's scientists. The guru was actually thought to have instructed Aum scientists to look into the specific Nazi method of producing sarin.

But whether or not the Hitler connection influenced Aum's use of sarin, Asahara's greatest passion had to do with nuclear weapons. Those were what he really craved. He was obsessed with them—as a potential victim of a nuclear attack to come, as a survivor of the atomic bombings of Japan, and as a fierce nuclearist who yearned to possess and use them.

His obsession began with Hiroshima. On a number of occasions he declared that Japan would experience "a hundred Hiroshimas," and many of his visions and "meditations" involved that city. In one of these visions he described traveling to Hiroshima on the "astral plane" and finding there grotesque evidence of a World War III nuclear holocaust that had already occurred. Always drawn to the most apocalyptic means of destruction, Asahara viewed chemical agents like sarin and biological agents like botulinus not only as "the poor man's nuclear weapons" (as many have) but also as "energy-saving nuclear weapons" (that is, highly effective without requiring the enormous explosive capacity of nuclear weapons or their elaborate production methods). Asahara also spoke with great enthusiasm about "laser weapons" and "plasma weapons," which he came to believe already existed and were even more powerful than the nuclear variety. But it was nuclear weapons that remained his measure and his passion.

Asahara and Aum represent an extreme case of what I call "trickle-down nuclearism," where smaller nations, cults, or transnational groups seek to obtain less expensive and easier-to-produce nuclear weapons. Trickle-down nuclearism is partly technological, having to do with the miniaturization of the weapons, the spread of knowledge about how to make them, and the improved technical skills of groups seeking them. But it is also a state of mind as the weapons, an ever longer-standing presence in our world, sink yet deeper into our sense of ourselves, leading to an intense yearning for and embracing of them as sources of ultimate power, especially on the part of those who imagine world-ending or world-purifying events. Over the course of the Cold War, most cults on the order of Aum Shinrikyo would not have imagined the possibility of acquiring nuclear weapons, but the above developments, combined with a failure on the part of prominent nuclear powers to rid themselves of their own stockpiles, have led nations and militant movements increasingly to equate possession of the weapons with international respect. The result has been an expanding sense of nuclear entitlement and an impetus toward proliferation.

One must recognize a remarkable trickle-down effect when such intense nuclear desire comes to permeate a cult like Aum, consisting of no more than 10,000 Japanese members and only 1,400 full-time "monks." It seems that "living with nuclear weapons" can have its hidden dangers, because increasingly smaller groups can develop strong impulses to live with them, too—and, in cases like Aum, to seek to possess them and then use them to end living in general. Formerly the United States and the Soviet Union had something of a monopoly, not just on the weapons but on the dangerous passions associated with them. Aum suggests that there is no limit to how far these passions can trickle down.

With Aum we may speak of a marriage between ultimate zealotry and ultimate weapons—or between an ideology of violent apocalypse and weapons with an apocalyptic essence. Each fed malignantly on the other: Aum's apocalyptic zealotry pushed it to seek the weapons, whose apocalyptic essence further intensified the zealotry.

APOCALYPTIC JAPAN

Japan, the society that gave rise to Aum, had experienced

an extraordinary degree of psychological and historical dislocation, dating back to its traumatic emergence from feudalism in the late nineteenth century. The struggles surrounding that dislocation culminated in devastating defeat in World War II, including something close to physical annihilation as well as a psychic collapse related to the breakdown of the emperor-centered religion that had so dominated the society. Indeed, the devastating saturation bombing of all of Japan's major cities, followed by the atomic bombings of Hiroshima and Nagasaki, created a uniquely apocalyptic wartime experience.

The behavior of the Japanese themselves during the war had its own apocalyptic dimensions. The extent of their wartime atrocities, never officially acknowledged in the postwar years, rivaled that of the Nazis. They included policies in China we would now call "ethnic cleansing"; the massacre and systematic rape of Chinese, notably in Nanking; slave labor on an unprecedented scale; extensive use of biological warfare; grotesque medical experiments on prisoners; the forcing of more than 100,000 women, mostly Korean, into prostitution to serve Japanese military personnel; and the systematic bombing of civilians in Chinese cities that some have viewed as a forerunner of Allied strategic bombing. The Japanese, that is, were apocalyptic perpetrators as well as victims.

The reverberations of that double experience have been evident throughout the post–World War II era. Underneath the seeming stability of Japanese society, there has been a powerful apocalyptic undercurrent, visible in novels, in popular cartoon *manga* narratives (or graphic novels), in films for television and movie theaters (of which the Godzilla series is the best known in America), and in wildly successful television shows. There are endless stories of the destruction or threatened destruction of the world and of postapocalyptic nuclear wastelands.

Nothing better indicates the apocalyptic explosion in Japanese popular culture than its strange embrace of the writings of the sixteenth-century French astrologer and physician Nostradamus, who loosely predicted (on the basis of the Book of Revelation) that the end of the world would come with the year 2000. Even looser Japanese translations of his work, some of which suggest that a savior will arrive from the East, have undergone more than 400 printings since 1973 and have sold in the millions, making the Japanese the world's greatest consumers of his murky message. Young Japanese were especially responsive to the extremity of that message because postwar society, though democratic in form, was perceived as authoritarian in its lockstep requirements and profoundly corrupt in its political and economic behavior. Many young and well-educated Japanese, in other words, were primed and ready to respond to the apocalyptic extremity of Shoko Asahara's message.

Also feeding Asahara's and Aum's extremity—and

appeal—was the nuclear drumbeat of the Cold War, and various threats by the United States and the Soviet Union to initiate something close to world destruction. After the end of the Cold War, Asahara found himself fascinated by the Gulf War of 1990–91. He identified with the Iraqi dictator Saddam Hussein, whom he saw as a nonwhite target of American aggression, but at the same time he was excited by America's high-tech, laser-guided weapons systems because they seemed harbingers of the Armageddon he so craved. As a late twentieth-century apocalyptic figure, Asahara associated Armageddon with the most advanced weapons technology; and as a paranoid and megalomanic guru close to madness, he was thrilled by the mass killing such technology promised. The ultimate lure for him, of course, was nuclear weapons, which conveyed to him the image that he alone—or with a few disciples—could achieve his ultimate goal of destroying the world.

AUM AND THE WORLD

Aum Shinrikyo was a cult that emerged from the apocalyptic underbelly of its own society. But I would emphasize that there was little that was uniquely Japanese about it. Certainly its impulse toward forcing the end, its fascination with Armageddon, and its attraction toward ultimate weaponry are increasingly common denominators in the global apocalyptic mindset and can take shape in any culture. Aum's Japanese circumstances probably caused it to go further in these areas than other groups previously had. (Since then Islamist and American extremists have more than caught up.) Rather than being unique, Aum epitomizes a category of cultic movement bent on world-ending violence.

Despite Aum's totalistic, one-sided sense of mission, its doctrine and practice were almost desperately eclectic and many-sided, contributing to what could be called apocalyptic multiculturalism. The cult was primarily Buddhist, but focused on elements of early Tibetan Buddhism closely tied to Hinduism. Asahara chose the world-destroying and restoring Hindu deity Shiva as his personal god and embraced the Christian Armageddon narrative as the basis for his apocalyptic vision. He referred as well to apocalyptic ideas in Hinduism and Buddhism, but these tended to be less precise and schematic than the Christian version, less of a road map to the end of time and more gradualistic depictions of spiritual and moral decline (though there is in Hinduism powerful imagery of Shiva dancing the cosmos into nonexistence in order to renew it).

The guru integrated some of his diverse religious elements by means of a personal vision in which Shiva instructed him to decode the Christian Book of Revelation, leading to his "discovery" that the book's "Son of Man" and Shiva were one and the same, that its description of the opening of "the sixth seal" actually meant the eruption of volcanoes including Japan's Mount Fuji, and that the book's reference to great fire, of course, meant nuclear war and an onrushing Armageddon. Asahara announced all of this to his disciples with great excitement and fervor.

In addition to its Tibetan roots, the Buddhism he practiced and taught had lively New Age components, including an emphasis on high states or "mystical experiences." Disciples whom I interviewed after the guru was arrested stressed to me how appealing this was, in contrast to the "deadness" of ordinary Japanese Buddhism, which had little to do with their life experience. The yoga Asahara taught quite skillfully had a similar combination of the very old and the very new. He was also influenced at least to some extent by a violently apocalyptic fringe of the American right, through translations of their writings distributed in Tokyo, though the virulent anti-Semitism he often expressed probably derived mainly from strong Japanese roots.

Such eclecticism has been common in "new religions" and cultic movements in Japan and elsewhere. Aum's version of eclecticism enabled it to be both ancient and current, as well as vastly inclusive in its claimed connection (however superficial or distorted) to much of the world's varied religious and cultural fare. This eclecticism contributed to an aura of universality, of being beyond any single religion or culture in its mission of cosmic purification.

Aum was eclectic in its finances as well. It was intensely focused on acquiring wealth, and made enormous amounts of money by aggressively merchandising its religion—selling ritual objects and literature, charging exorbitantly for initiations and practices, and requiring (sometimes through coercion and threat) that converts donate their total assets or those of their families—as well as through a great variety of businesses, such as computer companies, noodle shops and restaurants, bookstores, dating bureaus, and real-estate agencies. Such commercial enterprises, ordinarily considered by Asahara as part of Japan's cultural "pollution," became in Aum's hands a sacred form of service.

Everything was subsumed to the guru's murderous apocalyptic project (even if many followers were unclear about its exact nature or the violence it was to unleash), and such projects can generate extraordinary amounts of energy. The 1,400 or so full-time Aum religionists seemed to be everywhere, doing everything—conducting strenuous religious practices, manipulating other members, running profitable businesses, scouring Russia for ordinary and exotic weaponry, bribing officials, manufacturing and stockpiling and releasing chemical and biological weapons, threatening and sometimes killing people.

THE GURU AND HIS VISIONS
Megalomanic gurus tend to go through life with a sense of grievance or *resentment*, which in Asahara's case involved lifelong bitterness over having been sent to a school for the

blind. While he was indeed without vision in one eye, he was not legally blind since his vision was only partially impaired in the other, but he was sent to the school by his impoverished parents for reasons of convenience. (The school provided free tuition and board, and a completely sightless older brother had already been enrolled there.) While a guru's childhood can never completely explain his remarkable adult behavior, we can say that, as a boy, Asahara lived out, quite literally, Erasmus's dictum that "in the country of the blind the one-eyed man is king." In school, he proved manipulative and bullying, though he could also be tender to his completely blind followers. Even then he was extremely interested in accumulating money, intensely involved in drama (writing and acting in plays), and had grandiose ambitions that included becoming prime minister of Japan or at least a great doctor—all characteristics that were present in him as an adult.

He had a couple of brushes with the law, one soon after leaving the school, for causing bodily injury to another person, and one in Tokyo a bit later for selling fake medicines in a Chinese herbal pharmacy he had started. He entered the wide-open world of Japanese new religions in the early 1980s, joining a relatively established one before striking out on his own as a religious teacher and guru. He later described "achievements" of a kind generally required to create a guru's myth. These involved overcoming personal failures and psychological difficulties by spiritual means and, above all, experiencing cosmic visions, two of which were to become the basis for his guruism. At age thirty, he imagined himself leading an army of the gods to a victory of the forces of light over the forces of darkness; and the following year he achieved "final enlightenment" while meditating in the Himalayas.

In living out his impulse toward extremity, Asahara not only embraced the principle of "forcing the end," but developed an ideology of killing to heal, even of *altruistic murder* and *altruistic world destruction*. This was accomplished by "attack guruism" and "action prophecy," which combined lethal prediction with lethal action. The guru interpreted an ancient Buddhist principle called *poa* to mean that the killing of a person of inferior spiritual status by a person of high spiritual attainment was beneficial to the victim, enhancing his next rebirth and thereby his immortality. The more general principle here is that killing on a vast scale—whether by Aum, Islamist zealots, or superpower visionaries—is only possible when accompanied by a claim to virtue.

Asahara's one talent in life was being a guru, and he did demonstrate an ability to attract and hold disciples through intense and innovative forms of religious practice and mind manipulation. Asahara also revealed the complexities and contradictions that make up the mind of a guru (and the human mind in general): a man of superficial brilliance, he could be dignified and empathic, spiritually genuine, childish and inconsistent, fraudulent and manipulative, grandiose and schizoid, paranoid and delusional, megalomanic and murderous.

THE EXPERIENCE OF TRANSCENDENCE

The "mystical experiences" into which he guided disciples were generally induced by rapid-breathing exercises, which deoxygenated the brain and readily brought about altered states of consciousness, sometimes in combination with drugs and states of sleeplessness. This form of *experience of transcendence*, with or without drugs, is extremely important to apocalyptic groups, secular as well as religious. In the case of a cult like Aum, its apocalyptic component brings strong psychic energy to bear on whatever physiological state is created. Aum disciples embraced these high states to the point of addiction; they told me of ignoring or numbing themselves to evidence of duplicity and violence in the cult because they did not want to see or hear anything that might cause them to be denied access to their mystical experiences. Months or even years after leaving the cult, toward which they felt much disillusionment, they still longed for those lost mystical states, which, they repeatedly insisted, provided the most intensely satisfying spiritual moments they had ever known.

The exact state of the brain at such moments is not scientifically understood, nor can one be certain about the specific influence of an apocalyptic vision in rendering the oxygen-deprived "high state" still more intense (as compared, for instance, to the classical experiences of transcendence described by mystics). What one can say is that the mind/brain experience combined extreme euphoria with an impulse to struggle, even violently, on behalf of the special world (and the guru) promoting such euphoria.

The content of such experiences of transcendence is determined by the immediate environment, which, in Aum, meant images of the deified guru and of the expected apocalyptic event. Hence, there were frequent visions in which disciples, achieving one of Aum's ultimate aims, had a sense of merging completely with the guru. Another typical vision was that of a world in ruins with fires raging everywhere, a landscape without people except for a small group of Aum disciples, sometimes with the guru at its center, all of whom were quietly meditating.

THE "SOLE SURVIVOR TO RENEW MANKIND"

That postapocalyptic vision was key to the cult's overall project because in it Aum members become the *only survivors*, a tiny remnant of gentle but steadfast purity, ready to respiritualize a cleansed and vacant world—the kind of survivor remnant described in the Book of Revelation. There was in this a parallel to Pierce's vision in *The Turner Diaries* of the induced nuclear devastation of most of the world, leaving a remnant of white patriots, sharing in a similar steadfast and gentle purity and ready to repopulate the earth.

Such a postapocalyptic vision is reminiscent of a famous figure in the psychiatric literature who envisioned himself as the "sole survivor to renew mankind." The impulse, if acted upon, can become a form of addiction to continuous survival, and such addicts (as the Nobel Prizewinning writer Elias Canetti put it) "need corpses." The great majority of Aum disciples did not know that the cult was stockpiling biological and chemical weapons or seeking nuclear devices, but they were expecting an apocalyptic event and imagined themselves taking part in an "Armageddon-like battle" against evil forces. Only a few top disciples were privy to the guru's violent plans, though many others had a mindset that is sometimes referred to as "middle knowledge" (both knowing and not knowing) about any such violence.

In this sense the murderous side of Aum could be called its mystical secret—something on the order of Germans' knowledge of Nazi mass murder. Certainly everyone in Aum had a sense, however amorphous, that remaining loyal to the group was the only way to survive the cataclysm sure to come. For such a group, the sole means of survival becomes killing everyone else. That turned out to be a task beyond Aum's capacities, but the cult's combination of ultimate zealotry and ultimate weapons made it imaginable, and in acting on these imaginings Aum crossed a crucial threshold—from dreaming of or praying for Armageddon to vigorously attempting to bring it about.

CHAPTER 5

BIN LADEN AND AL–QAEDA—
"I ENVISION SALADIN COMING OUT
OF THE CLOUDS"

September 11, 2001, represented something new, a twenty-first-century globalization of apocalyptic terrorism. It was also a distillation of twentieth-century excess. Confronted with Osama bin Laden and al–Qaeda, I immediately thought of Shoko Asahara and Aum Shinrikyo. Others did too: Aum and its Tokyo sarin-gas attack were mentioned frequently in connection with the assaults on the World Trade Center and the Pentagon.

In many ways the two men and their organizations could not have been more different. Bin Laden came from a family of enormous wealth and influence in Saudi Arabia. He had access to higher education and worldly experience. Asahara's origins were in provincial poverty and an essentially claustrophobic educational and social experience. Equally important for us, bin Laden came to be the leader of a multinational organization with potential recruits and collaborators throughout the world, while Asahara was largely confined to a single relatively small cultic group. Bin Laden's monolithic immersion in the powerful Wahhabi version of Islam contrasts with Asahara's flamboyant religious eclecticism. The two men undoubtedly differ greatly in their psychological makeup as well, though we know too little about bin Laden to go far in such comparisons. While we may assume that he shares much of Asahara's grandiosity and some of his paranoia, he does not appear to be as precariously vulnerable to psychosis as the Japanese guru.

Yet whatever their differences, they and their organizations arrived at a similar cosmic impulse: that of active world destruction and re-creation.

ETERNAL JIHAD

What, then, does bin Laden want? He clearly has political goals. Along with a number of Islamists, he seeks to drive the American presence from the Middle East, weaken or destroy the United States, and overthrow various despotic or insufficiently Islamist regimes. But Americans find bin Laden confusing because, vast as these goals are, he seems to want something more. "Osama never interpreted Islam to assist a given political goal. Islam is his political goal," is the way one observer puts it. In fact, his focus is not just Islam, but an all-consuming Islamist perfection.

Beyond any political goal, he expresses a powerful, amorphous impulse to destroy a tainted world and renew it through Islamist purity. Rather than connecting their terrorist acts with precisely stated demands (for releasing prisoners or for publicizing their views), al–Qaeda leaders have typically made statements like "Our duty is to put an end to the humiliation of the people of Islam that has lasted too long," or "America thinks it is strong, that it controls everything, but what can it do, one day, against our young martyrs?" or "Our duty is to struggle against the enemies of God." Some view this vagueness as strategic, as it may to a certain extent be, but it also reflects the group's emphasis on apocalyptic, rather than specifically political, goals. All that is non-Islamic—or Islamic but considered inadequately so—must be eliminated. Al–Qaeda's ubiquitous enemies are both non-Islamics or "infidels" and Islamics deemed religiously lax or "apostates."

For bin Laden and other Islamist zealots, violence is part of a *jihad* or "holy war." The term has been used loosely, but suggests a struggle for Islam against those designated as its enemies. For radical Islamists, jihad is global and "a defense of the worldwide Islamic community." The grandiosity of such a project can easily blend into the apocalyptic. One observer believes that, with its 9/11 attacks, al–Qaeda crossed the line from being "utopian" (aiming at destroying and replacing the existing order) to apocalyptic (becoming "indiscriminate" in killing due to being "divinely ordained to commit violent acts")—all the while remaining "a very practical group . . . capable of chameleonlike maneuvering."

Recent scholarship suggests that the concept of jihad and the Muslim apocalyptic have always been closely connected. Jihad in Islamic religious writings normally emphasizes military action for the expansion as well as the defense of Islam, and although these writings contain little apocalyptic theory, there is considerable evidence "that Muhammad and his earliest followers . . . were moved to action by an overriding belief in the imminence of the Last Day." There was a related early belief that a struggle against a false Messiah at "the end" would usher in "the true messianic age." Similarly, jihad is referred to frequently as an "eternal state," and there is a tradition specifying that "jihad will continue until the sun rises in the west (which is one of the signs of the last days), when all people will believe, willingly or not." This "permanent jihad" was to be "the salvation of society."

The scholar David Cook sums up the historical overlap of jihad and apocalypse in a way that has great relevance for contemporary Islamists: "Jihad groups did not hesitate to make use of traditions in which the end of the world was prominent, and apocalyptic groups used the holy war as a means to express their essential ideological teachings."

But there has also been a nonviolent version of jihad, based on a statement Mohammed made to his followers after a battle, "We return from the lesser jihad to the greater jihad." The "greater jihad" came to mean the struggle against evil and imperfection in oneself, the struggle to be a better Muslim, or a better Muslim husband or wife or son or daughter. In that way, jihad became a psychological concept, an aspect of *inner* struggle in which individual aspirations can become bound up with visions of an all-consuming apocalyptic. Given the active principle of jihad as unrelenting holy war, there is some question about the viability of the nonviolent version. The very existence of the duality, however, suggests the power of the overall idea of jihad.

VIOLENT REJUVENATION

Precisely this duality was at issue in an influential booklet, *The Neglected Duty*, by an Egyptian, Muhammed Abd al-Salam Faraj, published in about 1980. Faraj was a member of the group responsible for the assassination of the Egyptian president Anwar Sadat in 1981, and drew heavily upon earlier theorists of radical Islamist movements. He argued that Muslim societies had declined because they had been lulled into believing that jihad was to be a nonviolent activity, and he insisted instead that the restoration of Islamic pride and power depended upon reclaiming the true meaning of jihad and establishing "the rule of God's Religion in our own country first." That meant concentrating on destroying the "near enemy," despotic apostate leaders who in his eyes had betrayed Islam, and only after that, the "far enemy," Israel.

Jihad should mean, Faraj claimed, "striving in the path of God," and the "neglected duty" of which he accused his fellow Muslims was failing to do so, by failing to engage in jihad as militant holy war. When one takes up that duty, "the punishment for an apostate will be heavier than for [one] who is by origin an infidel." As the scholar David C. Rapoport points out, such "sacred terrorists" believe their projects to be "sanctioned by divine authority, which humans have no right to alter." As in fundamentalist thought in general, the purification sought is modeled on a past of perfect harmony that never was, "the religion's most holy era, the founding period when deity and community were on the most intimate terms." This sanctified past becomes central to the apocalyptic vision. Guilt over one's "neglected duty" comes to include betrayal of the entire sacred tradition of Islam, and in this context one's personal struggle against evil and imperfection (the greater jihad) can only be carried out by engaging in the apocalyptic violence of holy war (the lesser jihad).

The principle of neglected duty put forward by Faraj drew heavily on the ideas of Sayyid Qutb, a former Egyptian government official whose extensive mid-twentieth-century writings, largely from prison, laid out much of what was to become the violent Islamist doctrine. Qutb wrote powerfully about *Jahiliyya*, originally a term for pre-Islamic seventh-century ignorance, which in his hands became a metaphysical category suggesting all that was corrupt, oppressive, and poisonous—that is, ultimate worldly pollution. This pollution, he believed, threatened the very existence of Islam, as did the Jews who "will be satisfied only with destruction of this religion [Islam]." Qutb's apocalyptic struggle entailed "a full revolt against human rulership in all its shapes and forms, systems and arrangements . . . It means destroying the kingdom of man to establish the kingdom of heaven on earth." There could hardly be a more direct rendering of the rationale for Islamist apocalyptic violence.

Bin Laden was much influenced by Qutb and Faraj but had a more immediate mentor in Sheikh Abdullah Azzam, his teacher, collaborator, and eventual rival. Azzam, a West Bank Palestinian, studied in Egypt and became a professor of Islamic law in Jordan and then Saudi Arabia, before emerging as the most prominent Islamic ideologist in the struggle against the Soviets in Afghanistan. Sometimes described as "the Emir of Jihad" or "godfather of global jihad," there was no nonsense about his focus on violence: "Jihad and the rifle alone: no negotiations, no conferences, and no dialogues." And that commitment to jihad was to apply everywhere as an obligation of Islamics "until all other lands that were Muslim are returned to us so that Islam will reign again." Azzam conveyed to bin Laden a fundamentalist vision of an Islamist theocracy or caliphate, and the two men worked closely together in Afghanistan to pursue that aim while resisting the invading Soviets during the decade from 1979–89. Azzam rallied support throughout the world for the Islamic resistance movement there with his fiery speeches and videotapes, while bin Laden distinguished himself as an organizer and financial supporter of the mujahedeen (holy warriors) and was mythologized as a fighter as well.

But by the late 1980s the two men had come into conflict, possibly over the focus of their movement: bin Laden favored a broad call to jihad against "apostate" Arab regimes, while Azzam emphasized jihad for Palestinians. In November 1989 Azzam was assassinated by means of a sophisticated car-bomb device, and although there had been many rumors about who might have been responsible (the Pakistani secret police; bin Laden himself), the killing has not been solved.

There has been some dispute about how significantly Arab fighters, as opposed to native Afghan warriors, contributed to the Soviet debacle, but there is no doubt that the victory was an intoxicating one for Islamists. Their miraculous success against a superpower—followed by the collapse of that superpower—could only mean that God had made them invincible. The considerable quantities of military equipment and financial support made available by the United States were dismissed in the exultant claim of (in Faraj's words) "jihad for the cause of god." More than any event, victory in Afghanistan contributed to an apocalyptic confidence on the part of Islamists: the existing world could be overturned and pure Islamist rule established.

Al–Qaeda emerged from bin Laden's Afghanistan experience. The name means "base" (or "database"), suggesting both its function as a hub for broader terrorist activities and its technocratic bent. Its identity was made clear from the beginning in its requirement of an oath of jihad and one of loyalty to bin Laden, its "emir." At the same time bin Laden drew together in the organization other high-level Islamists, such as Ayman al-Zawahiri, the Egyptian physician and leader in the Egyptian Islamic Jihad movement, who became one of his closest advisers. The group formed a working relationship with the Taliban, the extreme Afghan Islamist movement that took over the country, to which bin Laden provided considerable financial help. Al–Qaeda could set up its infamous training camps in Taliban-ruled areas and develop as an effective organization, although as outsiders its leaders had some conflict with the Taliban, and a few observers saw al–Qaeda as losing ground during the 1990s. Nonetheless, the group had embarked on its grandiose mission.

Bin Laden thus became part of a fervent Islamist movement of idealistic rejuvenation, a quest for collective pride, life-power, and purity, achievable only by violence. At its core was an impulse to reassert the health of Islam in a period of Arab stagnation—and so was but another version of killing to heal. This process of rejuvenation and "healing" took a quantum leap with the victory in Afghanistan. Since the United States actively armed and aided the Islamists as a Cold War project, we may say that America not only helped to create al–Qaeda but also played a significant role in the overall Islamist revitalization movement.

FATWAS OF PURIFICATION

Jihad can be formalized by the issue of a *fatwa* or legal decree. A fatwa can ordinarily be issued only by a *mufti*, a person with Islamic clerical standing, which bin Laden does not have. He has nonetheless issued two of them directed at America. This undoubtedly reflected both his authority within the radical Islamist movement (though others around him are believed to have considerable influence over him) and his personal grandiosity (though he later obtained clerical support to legitimize his *fatwas*).

The first of these, issued in 1996, broadly attacked the "Zionist-crusader alliance" (in Islamist rhetoric, "crusader" becomes an epithet for Western nations and groups now seen as enemies, invoking the historical memory of the Christian assaults on Muslim lands during the Crusades from the eleventh to the fourteenth century) and

"Zionist" is interchangeable with the "American-Israeli conspiracy." This fatwa, however, was aimed specifically at the post-Gulf War American military presence and bases in Saudi Arabia. Bin Laden declared that the "latest and greatest of these aggressions . . . since the death of the Prophet . . . is the occupation of the Land of the Two Holy Places [Mecca and Medina]." He was saying in effect that this defilement of the most sacred Islamic shrines by an American presence was an even greater violation than any taking of Islamic lives because those sacred places were crucial to the world's ultimate purification.

Bin Laden's second *fatwa*, issued in 1998, noted again the intolerable American presence "in the holiest of places" as well as "the great devastation inflicted on the Iraqi people" by the Gulf War of 1990–91, and by further American actions in the Middle East—all of which amounted to "a clear declaration of war on God, his messenger, and Muslims." Hence, he concluded, "the ruling to kill the Americans and their allies—civilians and military—is an individual duty for every Muslim who can do it in any country in which it is possible to do it." Any such acts would be in the service of liberating Mecca, the holy mosque, and other Islamic lands. This was "in accordance with the words of Almighty Allah"—which were to "fight the pagans altogether as they fight you altogether" . . . "fight them until there is no more tumult or oppression, and there prevail justice and faith in Allah."

These two *fatwas* extended an Islamic jihad/apocalyptic process by focusing on immediate political and military goals but also by merging them with the vision of a purifying cosmic upheaval. The way to connect these two levels was to confront America, the ultimate superpower, the personification of Western incursion and defilement.

BIN LADEN AND CHARISMA

Bin Laden and al–Qaeda are far from the whole story of Islamist terrorism. One knowledgeable observer speaks of "a broad movement of Islamic militancy that extends well beyond the influence and activities of any one man." But al–Qaeda has emerged as the boldest and most global of violent Islamist groups, and has been able to coordinate the actions of a number of them. Nor is bin Laden simply the king of all Islamist terrorists; on the contrary, he has been described as a man who is "impressionistic," constantly in need of a mentor, and still under the influence of older, more seasoned associates like Ayman al-Zawahiri.

Still, bin Laden has a special standing in his world as a charismatic leader. His legend continues to evolve as the tale of an extraordinarily rich man, well connected with Saudi royalty, who gave up all privileges and comforts to offer both his wealth and his person to the sacred struggle of the "mujahadeen" in Afghanistan. In this legend, as it grew, he became both a transnational Robin Hood and a bold military and spiritual hero who, more than any other

Islamist figure, could stand up to America. He did this in word and deed: attacks on the US embassies in Nairobi, Kenya, and Dar-es-Salaam, Tanzania in 1998, and on the destroyer the USS *Cole* in Yemen in 2000; probable connection with the World Trade Center bombing in 1993; and organizational leadership of the attacks on the World Trade Center and the Pentagon in 2001.

Adding to his charisma is his great height (six feet, five inches) and his indulgence in romantic, visionary prose and poetry. On a 2001 videotape released to his supporters, he spoke of how he "envision[ed] Saladin coming out of the clouds." Since Saladin was the great Islamic warrior-hero who in 1187 liberated Jerusalem from the Crusaders, bin Laden's vision undoubtedly has to do with a mystical sense of his own apocalyptic mission. Beyond Saladin, "bin Laden and his companions have been at pains to construct an image of themselves modeled on the Prophet Muhammed and his followers." His charisma has much to do with such associations and with his accompanying mission; for charisma, I would argue, is the capacity to transmit to others the sense that, if they follow you, their lives will take on new vitality and meaning, and they will become part of something eternal—precisely the heady feelings experienced by young Islamics attracted to bin Laden and al–Qaeda.

When his headquarters at Tora Bora in Afghanistan was destroyed by heavy American bombing, bin Laden managed to survive, escape, and issue a defiant message in which he taunted the Americans for their cowardice in not daring to employ their own troops to catch him. (They had used Afghan soldiers.) In the same message he declared that America could be defeated in Iraq by making use of "martyr operations," deep trenches, and urban warfare. Whether America's whirlwind military victory there caused bin Laden to lose any of his authority remains to be seen, as do the long-term effects of al–Qaeda's loss of its Afghan bases, a number of its leaders, and various material resources during the war in Afghanistan and other anti-terrorist activities by the United States aided by various European countries and Pakistan. The May 2003 terrorist bombing of an area of American and European living quarters in Riyadh, Saudi Arabia, thought to be associated with al–Qaeda, suggests that it has regrouped and is all too functional. At this writing, there is no reason not to assume that bin Laden remains a living charismatic Islamist figure bent on apocalyptic forays.

THE IMMORTAL DEAD

Islamist terrorists enter into a sacred drama in which they prepare themselves to join the immortal dead. They become part of a sanctified community of martyrs that includes all who have given their lives for the Islamic cause from the time of the Prophet. This sacred drama calls forth the authority of the heroic dead, and bestows that authority on the about-to-be-dead, who are absolutely purified and in the process earn an exquisite immortality.

This is quite different from martyrdom in battle, even a battle in which the odds are hopelessly against you. That martyrdom, though not passive—it can indeed be actively sought—and part of its own sacred drama, nonetheless depends upon what others do to you. Here the martyrdom is planned and embarked upon. The script, prepared well in advance, requires no action on the part of an enemy or "infidel" or anyone else.

The entire operation is viewed as a *ghazwah*, or "raid," a term that originated with the pre-Islamic nomads of Arabia and, beginning with the Prophet, came to be used for an attack on the infidel on behalf of Islam ("a raid . . . on the path of God"). The sacred drama of the raid, then, reaches back to the origins of Islam, and contemporary players can relive the heroic deeds of the Companions of the Prophet. As Hassan Mneimneh and Kanan Makiya put it, "It is as if men like Ali ibn Talib, the cousin and son-in-law of the Prophet, are going to be on the plane with Mohammad Atta, Marwan al-Shehhi, Ziad Jarrah, and the [other 9/11 terrorist attackers]."

Ancient martyrs are there, so to speak, to oversee and legitimate the unfolding drama. Should it be necessary to kill someone prior to the act of martyrdom (say, a passenger on a hijacked plane), that person is to be dispatched in the manner of a ritual slaughter. To carry out that slaughter is a sacred privilege: "A civilian passenger attempting to resist his hijackers is a gift bestowed by God upon the man chosen to kill him." Killing is not killing, but the enactment of a sacred script. Similarly, dying is not dying, but a step to immortality, as the hijackers' manual promises: "You will be soon, with God's permission, with your heavenly brides in heaven. Smile in the face of death oh young man. You are heading to the Paradise of Eternity." Indeed, that promise includes the "highest Paradise," which puts him "in the company of God." Behind these "highest" rewards and the extreme deeds for which they are given loom the highest apocalyptic stakes.

TECHNOCRATIC THEOCRACY

The sacred drama becomes a technical project, referred to as a "martyrdom operation." Spiritual energy and technology are hermetically combined within the martyrizing mind and the martyr-creating organization. Inclinations toward resistance or change of heart can be countered by the extreme psychological and social pressure exerted in the name of the sacred circle of martyrs, the immortal dead.

Groups like Aum Shinrikyo and al–Qaeda can at first appear to be thoroughly antimodern, at war with technology, science, and contemporary culture. But such apocalyptic movements often turn out to be uniquely modern amalgams, technocratic theocracies. Aum Shinrikyo actually had a kind of computer theory of the mind: the "bad data" from the culture had to be replaced by the "good data" from the guru. The cult made special efforts to recruit scientists, not only for weapons work but for studies that could demonstrate the truth of the guru's claims: for instance, electroencephalographic evidence of the effectiveness of meditation practices in slowing down brainwaves. Technique of every variety was embraced in the service of apocalyptic expectation.

Similarly, al–Qaeda showed its high respect for technology in hijacking sophisticated American jetliners and crashing them into the World Trade Center towers and the Pentagon in acts timed to make television history and clearly influenced by action and disaster movies. Its leaders, like those of Aum, assumed they were embracing technology only for its use in carrying out grandiose spiritual goals. But the matter is never that simple. In our time, technocratic impulses—whether related to science, the global media, or entertainment culture—are to some degree internalized by everyone, including members of apocalyptic groups, even though they may see themselves as defending ancient traditions against these very modern forces of impurity. Such groups, moreover, quickly relate contemporary technologies of various kinds to the desired apocalypse. Indeed, there is much that is technocratic in God's role in the apocalyptic scenario itself: systematic, protracted killing bringing about, first, world destruction, and then, world renewal. That blending of the technocratic and the mystical finds reverberations in the behavior of the American superpower.

The acts of September 11, 2001, combined a technocratic pragmatism with a strong sense of apocalyptic action. The vision of the project was not just bold but world-destroying. Consider the targets: the Pentagon, housing and symbolizing the world's most powerful military machine; the Twin Towers of the World Trade Center, symbolizing the world's greatest economy; and possibly the White House, symbolizing the presidential authority of the world's only superpower. The method—crashing the hijacked jetliners into these structures—was both transcendent and technically sophisticated (though containing more than a bit of Hollywood and of video-game fantasy). The American failure to anticipate these attacks was partly a matter of negligence and partly an inability to imagine at any level the apocalyptic dimensions of al–Qaeda's project. The apocalyptic aura created by the raging fires and the considerable destruction immediately surrounding the World Trade Center caused many people to think of either Hiroshima or Armageddon. That aura both contributed to, and was furthered by, the shock waves sent through the American economy (general recession, and the near collapse of the airline industry) and psyche, including painful struggles with vulnerability, and with aggrieved superpower status.

But 9/11 was not Hiroshima or Armageddon. Its

destruction was localized, confined to the area close to the World Trade Center, that surrounding the Pentagon, and the Pennsylvania site where the plane meant for Washington crashed. Nor can we say that the total of 3,044 deaths, grim as it was, qualified as an apocalypse. What we can say is that 9/11 expressed the farthest reach to date of Islamist apocalyptic martyrology.

Chapter 6
THE TERRORIST DYNAMIC

Immediately after the attacks of September 11, there was a widespread feeling among Americans that asking questions about the sources of, or trying to understand the roots of, Islamist terrorism was in bad taste—or worse. All that mattered was fighting back. If that feeling was understandable, it was also wrong-headed and made more so by the way the Bush administration used such reactions to advance its own agenda. Our leaders imposed a simple good-versus-evil global dichotomy on events and held to it, to the point of denouncing more nuanced reflection as "aiding the terrorists" or "unpatriotic." That kind of approach was a prescription for a narrow and militaristic nationalism and moralism.

To be sure, there is neither a single cause of Islamist terrorism—or any other kind, for that matter—nor is there a single relationship between it and any particular society.

History does not work that way; events and movements are inevitably overdetermined. We can, however, speak of a terrorist dynamic, a convergence of forces both psychological and historical that motivate and perpetuate behavior we designate as terrorism. That kind of model enables us to view al–Qaeda and related movements as many-sided, as, in fact, postmodern combinations of disparate elements: ancient Koranic doctrine recast and rendered Islamist; long-standing historical anger now directed at newly humiliating American incursions in the Middle East; contemporary worldwide fundamentalist and apocalyptic currents; anti-Western and antimodern impulses that have nontheless absorbed aspects of various Western ideologies as well as advanced technologies; and video and cinematic imagery drawing upon universal but mainly American-inspired popular culture. These influences have converged in a mission to depose existing regimes in Islamic cultural areas, attack the American superpower, and ultimately Islamicize the cosmos. The model suggests that Islamist terrorism is by no means "caused" by American policies, but also that American policies can have a considerable effect on the nature and scope of that terrorism.

Rather than attempt anything on the order of a full exploration of the terrorist dynamic, I will just suggest a few ways in which it operates, especially in connection with our country.

FRINGE AND CENTER

Important to the dynamic is the immediate relationship of a terrorist group to its society or social context. As with so much on this general subject, that relationship can often be paradoxical. For instance, Aum Shinrikyo was from all appearances a fringe group whose bizarrely murderous actions and visions seemed far removed from the lives, thoughts, and behavior of ordinary Japanese, no less from the scholars, students, writers, artists, and diplomats I had known over the years. So I was astounded to hear a talented young television producer say to me, "I feel myself to be Aum," and then, lest I miss his point, repeat the comment several times. It was not that he had any sympathy for Aum's violent acts. What he shared with Aum members, he explained, was much of their view of Japanese society as corrupt, repressive in its lockstep requirements and obligations, and intolerant of thought and behavior questioning existing norms.

That conversation suggested the kind of emotional contact that an extremist group—acting out forbidden impulses—could make with a society's mainstream, no matter how offended most might be by its violent behavior. The television producer did not say whether he was attracted to Aum's apocalyptic energies, which contrasted so strongly with the controlled, mundane routine of everyday life. Certainly some such attraction, along with fear and repulsion, must have been a factor in the fascination Japanese society and its media had with every detail of the cult's existence.

There was another curious response to the cult. A friend told me how, if someone began to reflect on large spiritual or philosophical questions, he might be told: "Don't be so Aum!" In one way, this response reflected the extent to which Aum had come to symbolize ultimate evil, so much so that one had to avoid resembling it in any way and was better off not becoming too spiritually inquisitive. But the remark could be ambiguous, double-edged in its irony, and suggest a critique of a society that had no place for reflection. It could even convey a measure of sympathy for Aum for raising significant questions. And then, somewhere between the fringe and the mainstream, one could find among Japan's angry youth stronger feelings of identification with Aum, whose continuing post-Tokyo-subway-gassing existence (with a change in name and a promise to eschew violence while at the same reasserting the spiritual "genius" of the imprisoned guru) remains a concern of the society.

In the Middle East, the multilevel connections between terrorists and their societies are no less complex and contradictory. Hamas, the Palestinian terrorist group, is a case in point. Its nurturing welfare projects and its murderous suicide bombings both hold places of esteem close to the heart of Palestinian society, so much so that Hamas is a formidable rival of Yasir Arafat, Mahmoud Abbas, and other leaders of the Palestinian Authority. The influence of Hamas is such that young suicide bombers are honored publicly by society; and their families, given monetary rewards, experience a rise in social status. Many in Palestinian society view the suicide bomber as having demonstrated the highest spiritual attainment. The martyr-hero quickly becomes part of legend, as well as a role model for others. This socialization of martyrdom, managed by Hamas organizers, comes to include children, to the extent that thirteen- or fourteen-year-olds begin to seek, and in some cases find, ways to have bombs strapped to them so that they can blow themselves up while killing a few Israelis. Little boys and girls, eight years old or even younger, aspire to do the same.

Yet among Palestinians there have been strong rumblings of discontent as well. Families cannot always hide their grief, which may emerge with some bitterness after the initial martyr-centered euphoria has passed. A prominent Palestinian psychiatrist has expressed strong misgivings about the "culture of death" surrounding suicide bombers, while Arab intellectuals and Palestinian leaders have become increasingly critical of the policy of suicide bombings, recognizing that they kill innocent civilians and reflect badly on Arab ethical standards. Evolving Arab awareness of the extremity and cost of suicide bombings—to young "martyrs" and their families, to Palestinian moral standing in the world and outside support for Palestinian political goals, and to the many Palestinians from all walks of life who suffer from the brutal Israeli military retaliation for each bombing—may serve to undermine the policy by withdrawing support from its orchestrators. A similar effect could be achieved by progress in a negotiated peace plan.

Yet suicide bombings continue, part of an entrenched policy drawn from a still-compelling Islamic focus on martyrdom. And it is clear that, even in those who are strongly against it, the suicide bombing strikes a deep emotional chord as a powerful response to feelings of helplessness and humiliation that have been so much part of Palestinian experience over these last decades.

THE MESSIAH AND OTHERS

From the Israeli side, one can observe in the murder of Yitzhak Rabin a different but not entirely unrelated contradiction. The murderer, Yigal Amir, a twenty-five-year-old student at Bar-Ilan University, would at the time have been considered by most Israelis part of the violent, unacceptable fringes of society. While he was not a member of a fringe cult like Aum Shinrikyo, he was a zealot immersed in the religion and politics of many varieties of Jewish messianism while enrolled at a major seat of learning known to harbor faculty and students with extreme views. But he was far from alone in his conviction that Rabin should be killed, in accordance with a long-obsolete principle of Jewish religious law found in the Torah, for interfering with messianic redemption.

The assassination took place on November 4, 1995, but for a period of more than a year before that, Orthodox rabbis in Israel and New York City had been discussing with approval this bizarre theocratic precept specifically in relation to Rabin. During his interrogations and in his writings, Amir told of contacts he had with rabbis who advocated the murder and signaled to him that it was all right to proceed. Over the same period of time, right-wing political groups, with their own visionary secular or religious convictions, were denouncing Rabin publicly as a "traitor" and "murderer." At demonstrations, some even created a photomontage of him dressed in an SS uniform, or carried coffins with "Rabin is murdering Zionism" painted on the sides.

The larger point here is that, while Amir would have been viewed by most Israelis as a fanatic, there were in existence religious, ideological, and political bridges between him and mainstream Israeli society. Again, we find that apocalyptic terrorists can connect with mainstream emotions, in this case fear and anger, and thereby influence a society's rhetoric and policies, including that which it comes to consider possible, even if not proper. (The Courage to Refuse movement mentioned earlier [Israeli soldiers refusing to fight in occupied territories] suggests a different kind of influence from a fringe position in society—a rejection of its own country's military terrorism. Though consisting of little more than 500 soldiers, their moral stance and their Israeli and Zionist credentials enable them to strike sympathetic chords in ordinary people in the mainstream of that society that could reawaken ideals of democracy and concerns about national decency.)

HUMILIATION

Al–Qaeda's transnational existence renders it different from these other examples. The group is based not on a struggle confined to any specific nation, apocalyptic or otherwise, but on a soaring concept of a pan-Islamic holy war meant to embrace the entire world. Even when operating in collusion with an Islamist government, the Taliban regime of Afghanistan, al–Qaeda's members were largely foreigners (Arabs rather than Afghans) who were using that country mainly as a geographic base and training area. With the American destruction of that base and the Taliban regime, al–Qaeda in a sense became even more itself, taking on the status of a secret, stateless, underground group. Its existence was perhaps more precarious, but its appeal, even among those who would never support it directly, could well have grown more intense, especially with the American invasion of Iraq.

Certainly much of the development of a group like al–Qaeda has to be understood in relation to Islamic history and tradition, just as violent American right-wing fundamentalists have to be understood in relation to historical Christianity, and violent right-wing Jewish religious groups in relation to historical Judaism. In each of those cases, however, the encounter with outside forces has had enormous importance.

With al–Qaeda, there is a legacy of confrontation with the West bound up with a sense of long-standing collective humiliation. Humiliation involves feelings of shame and disgrace, as well as helplessness in the face of abuse at the hands of a stronger party. These are among the most painful and indelible of human emotions. One who has known extreme shame and humiliation may forever struggle to recover a sense of agency and self-respect. Islamists' historical memory of the Christian Crusades that began in the eleventh century includes a strong element of humiliation, even though the Crusaders did not in the end triumph and Islam, led by the great culture hero Saladin, won many victories. Involved in that historical memory is the bitterness over the relatively primitive Christian Europe initiating a vicious religious and civilizational assault on Arab culture at its height. But with the triumph of European imperialism in the nineteenth century and the slow collapse of the Ottoman Empire, the experience of unadulterated humiliation took hold. It could be said to have culminated in the period at the end of World War I when France and England carved out the contours of the modern Middle East. But in another sense it has never ended.

After World War II, the creation of the state of Israel in the heart of the Middle East was experienced as a continuation of that ongoing humiliation at the hands of the West—as were the defeats of Arab armies in a series of wars with Israel, notably the 1967 conflict in which Syrian, Jordanian, and Egyptian armies were crushed and areas where Palestinians lived were turned into Israeli-occupied territories. Over recent decades, an increasingly aggressive American presence in the Middle East and the growth of our military bases throughout the region have been perceived by Islamics as more of the same. The Israeli invasion and occupation of part of Lebanon in 1982, the Gulf War of 1990–91 in which thousands of Iraqis were slaughtered, and the presence of American troops in Saudi Arabia—close to the two most holy Muslim sites of Mecca and Medina—continued a message of unending Islamic weakness. While historical feelings of humiliation have been manipulated by al–Qaeda leaders and others, it is fair to say that for more than 150 years that emotion has characterized much of the Islamic stance toward the West.

Islamics have sustained their numbers in the world (now on the order of one billion) but they have been otherwise overwhelmed by the West: militarily, technologically, and to a considerable degree, culturally. Islamics know themselves to be heirs to extraordinary past achievements—intellectual and scientific, artistic, political and religious—but the modern world has emerged mostly from an aggressively expansive West and the culture it exported with its weaponry and technology. The failures of Islamic governments—poverty amidst staggering undistributed wealth, corrupt institutions, despotic rulers—can easily be attributed by fanatical leaders like bin Laden simply to the humiliating hand of the West. And, of course, Western policies, historical and contemporary, have done much to feed that perception.

TEMPTATION AND DEFIANCE

After 9/11, it was frequently said by American politicians and pundits that Islamist terrorists attacked us out of sheer envy, that we are everything they wish to be. Such an assessment was obviously simplistic and self-serving, but there can also be no question that the temptation of Western culture, even for those theoretically opposed to it, presents a psychological problem of some complexity. In Mohammad Atta's letter to his fellow hijackers, he spoke of those attracted to Western culture as "the followers of Satan" and singled them out for special contempt: "These are the admirers of Western civilization, who have drunk their love for it and their hallowing of it with the cool water, and were afraid for their weak feeble stomachs." Atta and some of the other hijackers had lived in the West for considerable periods of time and, even while training for their suicide mission, had indulged in some of its secular pleasures: physical comfort, cultural and sexual experimentation, sports, alcohol, and drugs. To be sure, such pursuits are by no means exclusively Western, but they can be perceived as such, as they are in the writings of a number of radical Islamists. There can also be more profound attractions, having to do with forms of individual realization and relative freedom from hierarchy, however inconsistently practiced, and with cultural and economic achievements.

Exactly because it can seem so alluring, the impulse toward collective cleansing from this "temptation of the West" can be especially fierce, part of a painful internal struggle I have been able to observe in people in a number of non-Western cultures. What can result is a zealous return to an exaggerated version of one's own tradition and an equally zealous condemnation of all elements of this Western "taint." The quest for absolute cultural or religious purity can then readily blend with apocalyptic violence, which is the most extreme expression of radical breakout from the temptations of the West.

Beyond the rejection of such temptations, however, is the revitalizing experience of standing up to the West, particularly America. As Islamic observers friendly to the United States have said of bin Laden: "What he says and does represents what many [Muslims or Arabs] want to say and can't." He thus becomes "a symbol of defiance in the face of American arrogance." Bin Laden promises not just the end of Islamic humiliation, but the dramatic reversal of a centuries-old pattern: now it is the United States that is being humiliated. "What the United States tastes today is a very small thing compared to what we have tasted for tens of years . . . humiliation and contempt for more than eighty years."

Bin Laden's charisma is deeply intertwined with his flamboyant attempt to create a new pan-Islamic identity, a "new" self that is no longer to be the victim but the vanquisher, an aggressive warrior on a mission for God, armed and capable of humiliating the enemy. He can thus mobilize pan-Islamic idealism, which then becomes tragically channeled into murderous expressions of martyred violence. American war-making in response feeds the terrorist dynamic by reinforcing the Islamist claim to being engaged in a violent civilizational struggle.

The United States thus becomes crucial to that new Islamist identity as an Islamist version of the anti-Christ, a Goliath that must be slain along the way to an apocalyptic realization. This is the meaning of the American novelist Denis Johnson's comment on the terrorists: "They hate us as people hate a bad God, and they'll kill themselves to hurt us." Unfortunately, the "bad God" continues to behave in ways that heighten Islamic anger and feed apocalyptic fantasies.

Chapter 7
A SUPERPOWER'S "WAR ON TERRORISM"

Everyone knows about the more than 3,000 people killed on September 11, 2001, about the painful struggles of family members and other survivors, and about the overall economic and social disruption that followed. Less commented upon has been the American experience of humiliation. These attacks were carried out against the world's only superpower, in broad daylight, in front of television cameras, by a handful of barely armed terrorists who belonged to a small organization without even a claim to nationhood.

SUPERPOWER HUMILIATION

A superpower dominates and rules. Above all, it is never to be humiliated. In important ways, then, the "war on terrorism" represents an impulse to undo violently precisely the humiliation of that day. To be sure, the acts of 9/11 had a warlike aspect. They were committed by men convinced that they were at war with us. In post-Nuremberg terms they could undoubtedly be considered a "crime against humanity." The use of some kind of force against their perpetrators was inevitable and appropriate. The humiliation caused, together with American world ambitions, however, precluded dealing with the attacks as what they were—terrorism by a small group of determined zealots, not war. A more focused, restrained, internationalized response to al–Qaeda could have been far more effective without being a stimulus to expanded terrorism.

Unfortunately, our response was inseparable from our superpower status and the syndrome that went with it. Any nation attacked in that way would have felt itself humiliated. But given our national sense of being overwhelmingly powerful and unchallengeable, to have our major institutions violently penetrated was an intolerable, even inconceivable breach of superpower invulnerability, a contradiction that specifically fed our humiliation.

We know from history that collective humiliation can be a goad to various kinds of aggressive behavior—as has been true of bin Laden and al–Qaeda. It was also true of the Nazis. Nazi doctors told me of indelible scenes, which they either witnessed as young children or were told about by their fathers, of German soldiers returning home defeated after World War I. These beaten men, many of them wounded, engendered feelings of pathos, loss, and embarrassment, all amidst national misery and threatened revolution. Such scenes, associated with strong feelings of humiliation, were seized upon by the Nazis to the point where one could say that Hitler rose to power on the promise of avenging them.

With both al–Qaeda and the Nazis, humiliation, through manipulation but also powerful self-conviction, was transformed into exaggerated expressions of violence. Such psychological transformation from weakness and shame to collective pride and a sense of life-power, as well as power over others, can release enormous amounts of aggressive energy—a dangerous potential that has been present from the beginning of the American "war" on terrorism.

INFINITE WAR

War itself is an absolute, its unpredictable violence always containing apocalyptic possibilities. In this case, by militarizing the problem of terrorism, our leaders have dangerously obfuscated its political, social, and historical dimensions. Terrorism has instead been raised to the absolute level of war itself. And although American leaders speak of this as being a "different kind of war," there has been a drumbeat of ordinary war rhetoric and a clarion call to total victory and to the crushing defeat of our terrorist enemies. When President Bush declared that "this conflict was begun on the timing and terms of others

[but] will end in a way, and at an hour, of our choosing," he was misleading in suggesting not just a clear beginning to al–Qaeda's assaults but a decisive end in the "battle" against terrorism. In that same speech, given at a memorial service just three days after 9/11 at the National Cathedral in Washington, he also asserted, "Our responsibility to history is already clear: to answer these attacks and rid the world of evil." *Washington Post* reporter Bob Woodward, not a man given to irony, commented that "the president was casting his mission and that of the country in the grand vision of God's master plan."

At no time did Bush see his task as mounting a coordinated international operation against terrorism, for which he could have enlisted most of the governments of the world. Rather, upon hearing of the second plane crashing into the second tower, he remembers thinking: "They had declared war on us, and I made up my mind at that moment that we were going to war." Upon hearing of the plane crashing into the Pentagon, he told Vice President Cheney, "We're at war." Woodward thus calls his account of the president's first hundred days following 9/11 *Bush at War*. Bush would later recall, "I had to show the American people the resolve of a commander in chief that was going to do whatever it took to win." With world leaders, he felt he had to "look them in the eye and say, 'You're either with us or you're against us.'" Long before the invasion of Iraq—indeed, even before the invasion of Afghanistan—

Bush had come to identify himself, and be identified by others, as a "wartime president."

War-making can quickly become associated with "war fever," the mobilization of public excitement to the point of a collective experience of transcendence. War then becomes heroic, even mythic, a task that must be carried out for the defense of one's own nation, to realize its special destiny and the immortality of its people. In this case, the growth of war fever came in several stages: it began with Bush's personal declaration of war immediately after September 11, had a modest rise with the successful invasion of Afghanistan, and then a wave of ultrapatriotic excesses—triumphalism, and the labeling of critics as disloyal or treasonous—at the time of the invasion of Iraq. War fever tends always to be subject to disillusionment. Its underside is death anxiety, in this case related less to combat than to fears of new terrorist attacks at home or against Americans abroad—and later to growing casualties in occupied Iraq.

The scope of George Bush's war was suggested within days of 9/11 when the director of the CIA made a presentation called "Worldwide Attack Matrix" to the president and his inner circle, which described active or planned operations of various kinds in eighty countries, or what Woodward called "a secret global war on terror." Early on, the president had the view that "this war will be fought on many fronts" and that "we're going to rout out terror wherever it may exist." Although under consideration long before 9/11, the invasion of Iraq could be seen as a direct continuation of this unlimited war—all the more so because of a prevailing tone among the president and his advisers, who were described as eager "to emerge from the sea of words and to pull the trigger."

The war on terrorism became apocalyptic, then, exactly because it was militarized and yet amorphous, without limits of time or place, and because it has no clear end. It therefore enters the realm of the infinite. Implied in its approach is that every last terrorist everywhere on the earth is to be hunted down until there are no more terrorists anywhere to threaten us, and in that way the world will be rid of evil. Bush keeps his own personal "scorecard" for the war in the form of photographs, brief biographies, and personality sketches of those judged to be the world's most dangerous terrorists, each ready to be crossed out if killed or captured. The scorecard, he told Woodward, is always at hand in a desk drawer in the Oval Office.

Targeted as well are those who "harbor [the terrorists], feed them, house them," who are "just as guilty" and "will be held to account." That "Bush doctrine" was at one point extended by a Defense Department official, who spoke of "ending states who sponsor terrorism."

Any group or nation designated as terrorist or terrorist-supporting could thus be targeted by the war on terrorism. The looseness of that "war" was made clear when, on the day after 9/11, Donald Rumsfeld raised the question of invading Iraq. It turned out that a plan to do just that had been contemplated ever since the end of the Gulf War in 1991, and Rumsfeld, in advocating "going against terrorism more broadly than just al–Qaeda," was raising the possibility that America should seize the opportunity offered by 9/11 to mount such an attack. There was much subsequent discussion about whether Iraq, being the more "target-rich" adversary, was superior to Afghanistan as the war's first enemy. There was certainly an assumption that "the US would have to go after Saddam at some time if the war on terrorism was to be taken seriously." There were references, at first vague and later insistent, to alleged connections between Iraq and al–Qaeda, but it did not seem to matter so much that these connections could never be established.

WAR AND REALITY

The amorphousness of the war on terrorism was such that a country like Iraq, with a murderous dictator who had surely engaged in acts of terrorism in the past, could on that basis be treated *as if* it had major responsibility for 9/11. There was no evidence at all that it did. But in the belligerent atmosphere of the overall war on terrorism, by means of false accusations and emphasis on the evil things Saddam Hussein *had* done (for instance, the use of poison gas on his Kurdish minority), the administration succeeded in convincing more than half of all Americans that Saddam was a key player in 9/11.

The war on terrorism, then, took amorphous impulses toward combating terror and used them as a pretext for realizing a prior mission aimed at American global hegemony. The attack on Iraq reflected the reach not only of the "war on terrorism" but of deceptions and manipulations of reality that have accompanied it. In this context, the word "war" came to combine metaphor (as in the "war on poverty" or "war on drugs"), justification for "preemptive" (preventive) attack, conventional military combat, and assertion of superpower domination.

Behind such planning and manipulation can lie dreams and fantasies hardly less apocalyptic or world-purifying than those of al–Qaeda's leaders, or of Aum Shinrikyo's guru. For instance, former CIA Director James Woolsey, a close associate of Donald Rumsfeld and Deputy Secretary of Defense Paul Wolfowitz, spoke of the war against terrorism as a Fourth World War (the Third being the Cold War between the United States and the USSR). In addressing a group of college students, he declared, "This Fourth World War, I think, will last considerably longer than either World Wars I or II did for us. Hopefully not the full four-plus decades of the Cold War."

That kind of apocalyptic impulse in war-making has hardly proved conducive to a shared international approach. Indeed, in its essence, it precludes genuine sharing. While Bush has said frequently that he preferred to have allies in taking on terrorism and terrorist states worldwide, he has also made it clear that he did not want other countries to have any policy-making power on this issue. In one revealing statement, he declared, "At some point, we may be the only ones left. That's okay with me. We are Americans." In such declarations, he has all but claimed that Americans are the globe's anointed ones and that the sacred mission of purifying the earth is ours alone.

The amorphousness of the war on terrorism carries with it a paranoid edge, the suspicion that terrorists and their supporters are everywhere and must be preemptively attacked lest they emerge and attack us. Since such a war is limitless and infinite—extending from the farthest reaches of Indonesia or Afghanistan to Hamburg, Germany, or New York City, and from immediate combat to battles that continue into the unending future—it inevitably becomes associated with a degree of megalomania as well. As the planet's greatest military power replaces the complex world with its own imagined stripped-down us-versus-them version of it, our distorted national self *becomes* the world.

Despite the Bush administration's constant invocation of the theme of "security," the war on terrorism has created the very opposite—a sense of fear and insecurity among Americans, which is then mobilized in support of further aggressive plans in the extension of the larger "war." What results is a vicious circle that engenders what we seek to destroy: our excessive response to Islamist attacks creating ever more terrorists and, sooner or later, more terrorist attacks, which will in turn lead to an escalation of the war on terrorism, and so on. The projected "victory" becomes a form of aggressive longing, of sustained illusion, of an unending "Fourth World War" and a mythic cleansing— of terrorists, of evil, of our own fear. The American military apocalyptic can then be said to partner with and act in concert with the Islamist apocalyptic.

CHAPTER 8
APOCALYPTIC AMERICA

merica is "anointed" in another way. We have our own strong tendencies toward an apocalyptic mindset, which make us susceptible to the contagion of apocalyptic violence and quick to respond to such violence in kind. Relevant here is George Bush's polarization of the world into good and evil, his concept of the "axis of evil" to describe three nations considered antagonistic, and his stated goal of ridding the world of evil.

In the mindset of the president and many of those around him, our actions in the world, however bellicose and unilateral, are assumed to be part of a sacred design, of "God's master plan" (in Bob Woodward's paraphrase). The most dire measures are justified because they have been taken to carry out a divine project of combating evil. This Christian fundamentalist mindset blends with and intensifies our military fundamentalism. Together they have given rise to a contemporary American version of apocalyptic violence. The events of 9/11 did not create this combination but did enlarge it exponentially.

American apocalypticism is fed by the rhetoric of a president whose conversion to evangelical Christianity—administered by Billy Graham, America's leading evangelist—saved him from alcoholic self-destruction. Graham's son, Franklin, remains close to administration leaders, and has a tendency to be a bit more extreme than his father. When he recently called Islam "a very evil and wicked religion," the White House quickly dissociated itself from that view and he was forced to apologize, but he may well have been saying something widely believed by Christian fundamentalists, including some in the administration. (During the first Gulf War, when asked by Commanding General Norman Schwarzkopf to stop encouraging American troops to distribute Arabic-language New Testaments in Saudi Arabia, violating Saudi law and an American promise, Franklin Graham's answer was, "I'm also under orders, and that's from the king of kings and the lord of lords.") The "predominant creed" of the Bush White House, "where attendance at Bible study was, if not compulsory, not quite *uncompulsory*, either," has been "the culture of modern evangelicalism."

Bush's own religious convictions have been associated with dogmatic views and with tendencies toward personal and political fundamentalism. Certainly his administration has been friendly to Christian fundamentalism, which has provided much of his political base, and has embraced many of its passionately held social and political views: an antiabortion stand so extreme, for instance, that it has interfered with international aid programs, and sexual repression and homophobia so great as to block open scientific discussion of AIDS.

Among cabinet members, his attorney general, John Ashcroft, has views that approach the theocratic, declaring on one occasion, "We have no king but Jesus," a conviction not fully separable from his statements that those who raise critical questions about the war on terrorism "only aid terrorists."

"I'M IN THE LORD'S HANDS"

When the president spoke of 9/11 as "a great opportunity," he meant, among other things, an opportunity to take on evil and destroy it, and by making the war on terrorism a war on evil, he gave his spiritual energies, by his own testimony, a new focus. Before that, even being president had not seemed to fully engage him. But according to Woodward, in the wake of the attacks Bush became "consumed" by his "war," intent upon conveying to the American people that it was his purpose and "the nation's purpose," or, in his own words: "This is what my presidency is all about." To capture his new-found sense of mission, he came to use phrases like "I'm in the Lord's hands" and "There is a reason why I'm here."

Bush's intense religiosity undoubtedly further affects the psychology of his overall behavior. He characterizes himself as a person who wants everything to be clear and definite, who does not like to "nuance" things, or to deal with "lawyerly" arguments. Woodward describes him as a man who "wanted action, solutions," whose leadership style "bordered on the hurried," and he was told by Bush himself: "I know it is hard for you to believe, but I have not doubted what we are doing. . . . There is no doubt in my mind we're doing the right thing. Not one doubt."

Much of this is surely a long-held character trait and can be attributed to his psychological style or temperament: a tendency toward insisting on quick certainty as a means of suppressing, indeed annihilating, doubt. That tendency can be accompanied by a version of Texas macho that takes the form of the aggressive taunting of enemies (as in his recent "bring them on" challenge to Iraqi guerrillas who attack US soldiers), a stance he is said to assume particularly when under anxiety or strain. But both of these patterns may well be part of something more— of an overall religious worldview, within which he totalizes issues of right and wrong, truth and falsehood, good and evil. If one is carrying out a sacred task, then everything one does is part of a greater truth, part of a larger struggle for good and against evil. At one point Bush declared to Woodward, "I will seize the opportunity to achieve big goals." Such goals can approach the apocalyptic and lay claim to the ownership of truth. Bush's religious totalism may thus blend with temperamental inclinations toward doubt-precluding certainty and anxiety-relieving aggressiveness.

Could it be that not just the Islamists but our leaders, too, have goals that transcend the political, goals inspired by Christianity and buttressed by secular visions of American world control, and include a mystical belief in spreading our version of democracy and open markets—all of which is seen as ultimately a design of the Almighty, within which America can realize its spiritual calling? Bush recently may have given expression to his sense of receiving instructions from the Almighty in realizing that calling. At a small Middle Eastern summit meeting, he was quoted by Palestinian Prime Minister Mahmoud Abbas in the Israeli newspaper *Haaretz* as having said: "God told me to strike at al–Qaeda and I struck them, and then he instructed me to strike at Saddam, which I did, and now I am determined to solve the problem in the Middle East." George W. Bush has not himself created this mentality; it has strong American historical roots. But he and others around him exemplify and magnify our own marriage of zealotry and weaponry.

GOD AND HISTORY

That zealotry can readily enter into the kind of apocalyptic purpose expressed in the National Security Strategy of the United States, released by the Bush administration in September 2002, which called for military power unrivaled throughout the world and options of preventive and unilateral war-making where considered necessary. With such militarization of apocalyptic impulses, American policymakers move beyond mere religious dogma and into the kind of grandiosity and megalomania we have discussed. There are, after all, no limits to God's project. Since God's master plan is all-inclusive, the United States can continue to target not only the two remaining "members" of the "axis of evil" (Iran and North Korea) but any country our leaders designate as evil or dangerous. We are justified in this drive to control history and eliminate evil because ultimately it's God's plan, not ours.

One must consider as well the large reservoir of fundamentalist thought throughout America, as epitomized by two leaders of the movement, Jerry Falwell and Pat Robertson. Falwell blamed the attacks of 9/11 on such evil forces in American society as pagans, abortionists, feminists, gays, and the American Civil Liberties Union, all of whom caused God to "lift the curtain and allow the enemies of America to give us probably what we deserve." These two "American mullahs," as National Public Radio reporter Scott Simon called them, gravely and righteously warned of still greater disasters to come. Allying themselves with God's unlimited power to punish and destroy, they were more or less licking their theological chops in describing vistas of ever-greater devastation that could lead to the yearned-for "end time": to God's destruction of the world preceding the return of Jesus. Within this worldview, apocalyptic violence can be accepted, even welcomed, as a means of cosmic purification. Millions of Americans hold aspects of such a worldview, including some in positions of political leadership, though often in confused and contradictory ways.

A similar worldview was held by seventeenth-century Puritans, who considered the suffering and dying they experienced in their wars with the Indians as God's punishment for religious backsliding in their own second generation, and his judgment on their sins. The historian of American violence Richard Slotkin has described these events as a "holy war" intended to realize "the concept of New England as the new Israel, the new abiding place of a newly chosen race." For the individual Puritan, violent conquest of the Indians meant "conquering the forces of sin within the body politic or in his own mind." This "regeneration through violence" was based on an apocalyptic vision of the "new Israel," but included as well powerful forms of individual revitalization—of new energy and purpose—that were both psychological and religious.

Falwell and Robertson have engaged in no such violence. But one must ask whether fundamentalists within the Bush administration, who *are* engaging in violence, do not at some psychological level envision the war on terrorism as a vehicle for our own salvation, for a new American regeneration through violence, for not only destroying evil worldwide but cleansing ourselves of our own sins and revitalizing our spiritual energies through our predominant military power.

Woodward ends his book on Bush on a mystical note. He describes a scene in which twenty-five men from different Special Forces and CIA teams gather at a desolate site in Afghanistan, where they have arranged a pile of rocks as a tombstone over a buried piece of the demolished World Trade Center. One of the men leads a prayer as others kneel, consecrating the spot as a memorial to the dead of September 11, and then declares: "We will export death and violence to the four corners of the earth in defense of our great nation." Woodward presents the scene as depicting the determination of an aggrieved nation to strike back. But it also suggests a sequence leading from memorialization to self-defense to apocalyptic militarism.

Such fundamentalist and apocalyptic tendencies by no means determine all of American policy, which can alternate with inclinations toward pragmatic restraint. But impulses toward regeneration through apocalyptic violence are an ever-present danger.

The Bush administration should by no means be seen as a mirror image of bin Laden or Islamism. Rather it is part of an ongoing dynamic in which the American apocalyptic interacts, almost to the point of collusion, with the Islamist apocalyptic, each intensifying the other in an escalating process that has in it the potential seeds of world destruction.

CHAPTER 9
SUPERPOWER VULNERABILITY

I t is almost un-American to be vulnerable. As a people, we pride ourselves on being able to stand up to anything, solve all problems. We have long had a national self-image that involves an ability to call forth reservoirs of strength when we need it, and a sense of a protected existence peculiar to America in an otherwise precarious world. In recent times we managed, after all, to weather the most brutal century in human history relatively unscathed.

THE BLESSED COUNTRY

Our attitude stems partly from geography. We have always claimed a glorious aloneness thanks to what has been called the "free security" of the two great oceans which separate us from dangerous upheavals in Europe and Asia. While George Washington was not the isolationist he is sometimes represented to be, he insisted in his celebrated Farewell

Address of 1796, "'Tis our true policy to steer clear of permanent alliances, with any portion of the foreign world." That image has been embraced, and often simplified or distorted, by politicians ever since. (He warned against *permanent* alliances, not alliances in general.)

The idea of our separateness and safety from faraway conflicts has had importance from the time of the early settlers, many of whom left Europe to escape political, religious, or legal threats or entanglements. Even if one came as an adventurer or an empire-builder, one was *leaving* a continent of complexity and conflict for a land whose *remoteness* could support new beginnings. Abraham Lincoln absolutized that remoteness and security from outside attack in order to stress that our only danger came from ourselves: "All the armies of Europe, Asia and Africa combined, with all the treasure of the earth (our own excepted) in their military chest; with a Buonaparte for a commander, could not by force, take a drink from the Ohio, or make a track on the Blue Ridge, in a trial of a thousand years." However much the world has shrunk technologically in the last half century, and however far-ranging our own superpower forays, that sense of geographic invulnerability has never left us.

We have seen ourselves as not only separate from but different from the rest of the world, a special nation among nations. That sense of *American exceptionalism* was intensely observed by Alexis de Tocqueville, the brilliant

French politician and writer, in the early nineteenth century. In de Tocqueville's view of America, "A course almost without limits, a field without horizon, is revealed: the human spirit rushes forward and traverses [it] in every direction." American exceptionalism has always been, as the sociologist Seymour Martin Lipset has pointed out, "a double-edged sword." In the psychological life of Americans it has been bound up with feelings of unique virtue, strength, and success. But this has sometimes led Americans to be "utopian moralists, who press hard to institutionalize virtue, to destroy evil people, and eliminate wicked institutions and practices." That subjective exceptionalism has been vividly expressed in the historian Richard Hofstadter's observation, "It has been our fate as a nation not to have ideologies, but to be one."

At the time of the Puritans, sentiments of exceptionalism were expressed in biblical terms: America was an "Arcadian image of the New World . . . an Eden from which the serpent and forbidden trees had been thoroughly excluded," and "a new Promised Land and a New Jerusalem." The language was that of a postapocalyptic utopia, and remnants of such sentiments persist whenever we speak of ourselves in more secular terms as the "new world."

Important to this feeling of exceptionalism has been a deep sense that America offered unparalleled access to regenerative power. As Richard Slotkin explains: "The first colonists saw in America an opportunity to regenerate their fortunes, their spirits, and the power of their church and nation," though "the means to that regeneration ultimately became the means of violence." Even when Americans played what has been called a "shell game of identity," they could experience an unlimited capacity for renewal—endless new beginnings as individuals or as a nation.

Slotkin speaks of a new relationship to authority in this new world. While "in Europe all men were under authority; in America all men dreamed they had the power to become authority." These claims of new authority extended to the country as a whole, to America's authority among nations—a claim to new national authority that was expanded over time thanks to America's considerable achievements—economic, technological, scientific, and cultural.

American exceptionalism has often had the overall psychological quality of a sense of ourselves as a *blessed people*, immune from the defeats and sufferings of others. But underneath that sense there had to be a potential chink in our psychological armor—which was a deep-seated if hidden sense of vulnerability.

OMNIPOTENCE AND VULNERABILITY

Ironically, superpower syndrome projects the problem of American vulnerability onto the world stage. A superpower is perceived as possessing more than natural power.

(In this sense it comes closer to resembling the comic-strip hero *Superman* than the Nietzschean *Superman*.) For a nation, its leaders, or even its ordinary citizens to enter into the superpower syndrome is to lay claim to omnipotence, to power that is unlimited, which is ultimately power over death.

At the heart of the superpower syndrome then is the need to eliminate a vulnerability that, as the antithesis of omnipotence, contains the basic contradiction of the syndrome. For vulnerability can never be eliminated, either by a nation or an individual. In seeking its elimination, the superpower finds itself on a psychological treadmill. The idea of vulnerability is intolerable, the fact of it irrefutable. One solution is to maintain an *illusion of invulnerability*. But the superpower then runs the danger of taking increasingly draconian actions to sustain that illusion. For to do otherwise would be to surrender the cherished status of superpower.

Other nations have experiences in the world that render them and their citizens all too aware of the essential vulnerability of life on earth. They also may be influenced by religious and cultural traditions (far weaker in the United States) that emphasize vulnerability as an aspect of human mortality. No such reality can be accepted by those clinging to a sense of omnipotence.

At issue is the experience of death anxiety, which is the strongest manifestation of vulnerability. Such a deep-seated sense of vulnerability can sometimes be acknowledged by the ordinary citizens of a superpower, or even at times by its leaders, who may admit, for instance, that there is no guaranteed defense against terrorist acts. But those leaders nonetheless remain committed to eliminating precisely that vulnerability—committed, that is, to the illusory goal of invulnerability. When that goal is repeatedly undermined—whether by large-scale terrorist acts like 9/11, or as at present by militant resistance to American hegemony in Iraq and elsewhere in the Middle East—both the superpower and the world it acts upon may become dangerously destabilized.

NUCLEAR "CREATIVITY"

Nuclear weapons lie at the core of superpower status. Large stockpiles of such weaponry—and the American arsenal contains about 10,000 nuclear warheads—provide an apocalyptic dimension to projections of force and threatened destruction. A superpower must not only be dominant in the nuclear arena but such dominance becomes a focal aspect of its self-definition.

That kind of weapons-centered self-definition has been embraced more single-mindedly by George W. Bush than by any previous American president. Every nuclear-age president, beginning with Harry Truman, has struggled with the painful contradiction that surrounds nuclear weapons. On the one hand, each president on some occasion affirmed America's right to use them—that is, to treat them as if they were ordinary weapons should such use be judged necessary for the national interest; hence no American administration has been willing to sign a no-first-use agreement. On the other hand, each president has also expressed the view that these weapons are so destructive, so grotesque in their human effects, that they should in fact be considered unusable.

This latter stance has represented at least a partial taboo, a sense that there is a barrier between the most destructive "conventional weapons" and nuclear devices, a barrier that should not be crossed. However partial, that taboo has had enormous value in suggesting that, with nuclear weapons, one is dealing with a special category of infinite destruction. It is a taboo that has—if in a few cases barely—held since the American atomic bombing of Nagasaki on August 9, 1945.

But President Bush and his advisers have expressed no such ambivalence about the weapons. His administration's nuclearism has been overt and unfettered. His nuclear strategists have sought to discover ever more creative uses for the weapons. For instance, in their Nuclear Posture Review of December 2001, they spoke of developing small nuclear warheads called "Robust Nuclear Earth Penetrators" (also known as "bunker busters") for potential use against North Korea's underground caves. And more recently the administration has contested a ban on the use of low-yield nuclear weapons that had been in effect since 1993, and encouraged American nuclear scientists to explore new generations of such weaponry whose lower yield would make them more usable. They have also made plans for lofting nuclear and other advanced weaponry into the last demilitarized "frontier," that of space, and have indicated that they are eager to resume the underground nuclear testing that has been in abeyance since 1992.

The administration has, in fact, managed to give nuclear weapons increasing value globally as the currency of power; its actions in the Middle East and East Asia have provoked Iran and North Korea to accelerate their own nuclear programs and could, by a kind of domino effect, contribute to the nuclear arming of other countries, including Japan. This unapologetic nuclearism has undoubtedly been a way of countering the superpower fear of vulnerability, and nowhere is that vulnerability more intolerable than in association with others' nuclear weapons.

The pattern is ominous because nuclear proliferation, including the phenomenon of trickle-down nuclearism, is a reality of the post-Cold War "second nuclear age." The Bush administration has been aware of this danger, but tends to focus on a policy of "counter-proliferation," which includes the possibility of military attacks on countries that possess or are in the process of acquiring the weapons and are deemed unstable or antagonistic to the

United States. The administration has also threatened to use nuclear weapons on anyone who uses weapons of mass destruction against the United States (a threat that was made to Iraq in the prewar months in connection with its possible use of chemical or biological weapons).

American leaders went further. They justified the preventive attack on Iraq with the claim that it was illegally stockpiling weapons of mass destruction. And while there was certainly a grand imperial design behind the war, the superpower fear of others' weapons of mass destruction was at issue as well. To be sure, the manipulative American presentations of "evidence" for Iraqi weapons of mass destruction (including the citing of crudely forged documents that supposedly revealed Iraqi uranium purchases in the African country of Niger) were largely a pretext for an invasion the Bush administration had long been determined to carry out. But the need to preserve the illusion of invulnerability also played its part, contributing to a self-proclaimed entitlement to head off imagined future dangers, including the possibility that Saddam Hussein might provide al–Qaeda with nuclear weapons (although Iraq has had no functional nuclear program since the early 1990s). In that sequence, a declared "preemptive" war became a preventive war which in turn became a "counter-proliferation" war.

In this way the approach to the very real problem of nuclear proliferation was thoroughly militarized, and itself rendered potentially nuclear. Ultimately, the only superpower finds it difficult to tolerate anyone else possessing such weapons, and no less difficult to imagine a world in which it might surrender its own nuclear arsenal. As one American official was quoted as saying, when asked about proliferation, "My ideal for the perfect number of nuclear-weapons states is one."

Superpower nuclearism and "counter-proliferation," are, not surprisingly, likely to have psychological and political effects quite different from those intended. Smaller nations at odds with the United States, becoming painfully aware of their own vulnerability and their potential humiliation in the face of a possible attack, are then drawn to their own version of nuclearism—to nuclear magic—as a source of power and pride. And they can point to evidence for doing so: Iraq, lacking a nuclear program, was invaded; North Korea, with a relatively advanced one, was not. Of course, such an approach could also hasten an American attack.

Nuclearism is contagious, and the supernatural power it seems to bestow is inseparable from a deepening fear of vulnerability. During the Cold War, this paradox of supernatural power and profound vulnerability was the crux of the interaction between the United States and the Soviet Union. America's ever newer generations of nuclear weapons and strategies made the Soviets feel sufficiently vulnerable to counteract them with no less threatening stockpiles and strategies, which in turn intensified American feelings of vulnerability, which led to further stockpiling and more aggressive strategies until the arsenals of the two superpowers reached absurd levels, quite capable of destroying planet Earth and more.

Now, with just one superpower but many more actual or aspiring nuclear nations, the process has become much more amorphous and considerably less manageable. Intolerant of its own vulnerability, and dismissive of diplomatic arms-control approaches, the Bush administration is now on the lookout everywhere for weapons of mass destruction—especially those actually or potentially in the hands of unfriendly nations or terrorist groups. Such weapons may be manufactured, purchased, or stolen; or low-tech forms of attack may be mounted that are aimed specifically at the superpower's own nuclear weapons and energy installations. The superpower, trapped in its syndrome, finds itself with little recourse but the endless use of force.

Unmitigated nuclearism combined with a quest for exclusive control of the nuclear arena can only enhance the weapons' standing as a currency of power everywhere, creating a vicious circle of action and reaction from which there appears to be no exit. The seemingly invincible nation can never rest, facing as it does an ever-widening, ever-escalating arena of threats, which span the world and could destroy it. More than any other nation, the superpower is psychologically bedeviled by vulnerability.

CHAPTER 10
AMERICANS AS SURVIVORS

s a result of 9/11, all Americans shared a particular psychological experience. They became survivors. A survivor is one who has encountered, been exposed to, or witnessed death and has remained alive. The category extends to those who were far removed geographically from the World Trade Center and the Pentagon, because of their immersion in death-linked television images and their sense of being part of a painful national ordeal that threatened their country's future as well as their own. How people deal with that death encounter—the meaning they give it—has enormous significance for their subsequent actions and for their lives in general. To consider how Americans have responded to 9/11, we need to identify certain common themes that occur regularly in the psychology of the survivor.

DEATH ANXIETY

The most immediate theme is that of the *death imprint* and related *death anxiety*. In the case of 9/11, those close to the World Trade Center or the Pentagon retained images of people dying grotesquely—some of them jumping to their deaths—amid the fires and the collapsing buildings. These images were briefly disseminated by the media, but were quickly considered too gruesome and replaced by the larger spectacle of hijacked planes crashing into the towers and the towers themselves crumbling—certainly profoundly impressive, often overwhelming, at the same time strangely remote and almost lacking in human content. Their constant repetition inevitably diminished their impact, even as it sustained Americans' overall sense of catastrophe.

Such indelible images can stay with one over a lifetime. When Hiroshima survivors told me, in 1962, about the experiences they had undergone seventeen years before, their descriptions were so powerful I felt as if they had brought the atomic bomb into the small office in which we sat. They were also affected by the realization that what had caused their suffering was not a "natural disaster" but something done to them by other human beings. That was no less true of survivors of the World Trade Center, though the dimensions of the disaster were in no way comparable to Hiroshima.

A survivor's death anxiety includes fear of a recurrence of the disaster. Hiroshima survivors feared another bomb of similar magnitude—this time, rumor had it, an "ice bomb" that would freeze the entire city and everyone in it (in contrast to the "hot bomb" that had caused the city to erupt in flames). The feeling was that those who had made and used such an extraordinary weapon could be capable of *any* form of destructiveness. In the wake of 9/11, there have been similar widespread fears and fantasies about likely targets of a terrorist recurrence—bridges, tunnels, or subways in New York or possibly San Francisco, or tall buildings in Chicago—and likely weaponry, such as "dirty bombs" (combining a conventional explosive core with an outer layer of radioactive material), anthrax spores or smallpox virus, or sarin gas (on the model of Aum Shinrikyo).

But unlike the situation of Hiroshima survivors, the forms of 9/11 recurrence feared are all too plausible, based on more or less reasonable estimates of terrorist capabilities. "Dirty bomb" fears connect New Yorkers (and other Americans) with Hiroshima in a dread of invisible contamination from radiation effects. That dread could potentially envelop an entire city, should such a bomb be detonated, however limited its physical impact.

By and large, the nearer one was to the attack—whether at the World Trade Center or the Pentagon—the greater one's death anxiety. The fear level in New York City differed considerably from that in most other parts of the country, as indicated by studies of trauma symptoms there. But elements of death anxiety span the United

States, affecting leaders and ordinary people alike, linking the two in what could be called a common pathway of vulnerability. However muted, such anxiety and vulnerability do not disappear.

DEATH GUILT

Survivors find it difficult to avoid feelings of self-condemnation or what I call *death guilt* (frequently termed "survivor guilt"). One may also speak of paradoxical guilt—experienced inappropriately, so to speak, by victims, while the perpetrators call forth various psychological mechanisms to diminish or eliminate such feelings, especially if their killing is done for a sacred cause.*

Death guilt has to do with others dying and not oneself, or with remaining alive when one had been close to death (and was "supposed" to die). It has to do with what I call *failed enactment:* one's inability at the moment of the disaster to act in the way one would have expected of oneself (saving people, resisting the perpetrators), or even to have experienced the expectable and appropriate emotions (strong compassion for victims, rage toward perpetrators). Death guilt begins with, and is sustained by, this "failure"; the memory can be endlessly replayed psychologically,

---

*There has been much confusion over "survivor guilt" and related terms because they can be erroneously understood to suggest actual wrongdoing, as opposed to guilt *feelings*, which are psychological manifestations of self-condemnation, however undeserved.

and although somewhat ameliorated over time, is never completely erased.

Guilt feelings are closely bound up with a sense of debt to the dead, a debt that can never quite be repaid. Such feelings can contain the implication, however illogical, that others' deaths were exchanged for one's own, that one is alive because someone else died.

Death guilt haunts the survivor, sometimes in ways that can be expressed only in dreams. A young woman who had been close to the World Trade Center on 9/11 recounted to me a painful dream in which she watched from the street as people jumped to their deaths from a high building. In the dream she experienced a troubled feeling that she should find a way to help those people. When she awoke she realized that the dream reminded her of something she had completely "forgotten": namely, that she had actually witnessed people jumping from the Twin Towers and had suppressed the memory along with accompanying feelings of self-condemnation.

Death guilt has to do with our sense of responsibility, as cultural animals, to help others stay alive, even when they are strangers. We can speak of an animating form of guilt, as some Vietnam veterans experienced, when self-condemnation is transformed into a sense of responsibility to oppose violence and enhance life. But death guilt can be volatile and destructive when suppressed, and can be transformed instead into impulses toward further violence.

PSYCHIC NUMBING

Equally primal in survivors is the struggle over how much to feel. Hiroshima survivors told me how, at the time the bomb fell, they were aware of the sea of death around them but, almost immediately, simply ceased to feel. Their emotions were switched off. One survivor described it as a "paralysis of my mind." I called it *psychic closing off* and as a general phenomenon, *psychic numbing*. By psychic numbing I mean the inability, or disinclination, to feel, a freezing of the psyche. This is a response in humans analogous to the freezing response animals sometimes have in relation to threat or danger. It could be understood as a temporary death in the service of remaining psychically or even physically alive. It allows one to function cognitively without responding emotionally to a scene so extreme that it might otherwise be hard to stay sane. Psychic numbing can be highly adaptive to survivors of death encounters; it can also enable perpetrators to do their dirty work.

But feelings, of course, do break through. Those who have studied survivors of 9/11 have described "zones of sadness," with the most intense forms of both numbing and grief taking place among those who found themselves in the areas closest to Ground Zero. Reactions are by no means entirely predictable, however, and there have been strong responses of numbing and grief in places quite distant from the Twin Towers or the Pentagon, influenced not only by prior psychological inclinations but by connections of some kind with the targets or victims of 9/11, and by religious beliefs and political ideologies. Immediate psychic numbing can later give way to enhanced sensitivity and responsiveness, or it can extend into depression, withdrawal, or aggressive behavior.

The repeatedly televised images of planes crashing into the Twin Towers, powerful as they were, could seem wildly fantastic, almost imaginary or "virtual" in their distance from individual death and suffering. Subsequent images did convey pain and loss but the coverage, as intense as it was, proved narrow, providing little in the way of cause or meaning. One could say that Americans were brought into the 9/11 experience in a way that was both vividly actual and unreal. Yet struggles with feeling and not feeling took place nationwide.

SUSPICIOUSNESS

Survivors can be alert to issues of authenticity, and may be suspicious of the intentions of others. This suspiciousness can manifest itself in edgy rivalries and conflicts over eligibility for help, as occurred in Hiroshima and in New York, and is in fact an aspect of any disaster. Another important matter for survivors is that of autonomy, of overcoming the helplessness experienced during their death encounter. Survivors often feel in need of help, but may perceive any help offered as a reminder of weakness (as experienced at the time and subsequently). Financial help may be sought but treated uneasily as "blood money." Instead of paying one's debt to the dead, it can seem that one is receiving payment from them.

All of this is part of a struggle to overcome the *counterfeit universe* to which survivors were exposed during their death encounter, a universe of moral inversion in which large-scale killing and absurd dying were the norm. They can find it extremely difficult to believe in the efforts of anyone, certainly those of uncomprehending outsiders, to restore a moral universe. In the process, some survivors can become newly aware of ethical distinctions in their lives, but many others experience instead profound suspiciousness toward the outside world and a deep reluctance to engage in cooperative enterprises.

MEANING AND MISSION

The overall task of the survivor is to find meaning in his or her ordeal. We are meaning-hungry creatures, and what has been devastatingly chaotic must be given form. Only by finding meaning in the death encounter can one find meaning in the rest of one's life.

No war or disaster, however extreme, provides meaning in itself. That meaning must be constructed by survivors or others who have been affected. What such a disaster does do is infuse any constructed meaning with life-and-death dimensions, which in turn can be passionately fused with ultimate values.

The actual meanings derived from any disaster can vary wildly. Consider, for instance, two survivor meanings drawn by Jews from the Holocaust. There is that of Meir Kahane, an American-born, later Israeli, political extremist and third-generation rabbi, whose slogan "Never again!" became the basis for the fascist-like political group he created, the Jewish Defense League. Its policies included the ready labeling of Arabs as Nazis and the encouragement of the use of violence toward anyone seen as an enemy of Israel or of the Jews. In striking contrast, a small group of Holocaust survivors came together in 1969 to protest the American slaughter of about 500 Vietnamese civilians in the village of My Lai. They told me that My Lai came too close to their own experience, and the meaning they drew from that experience was that systematic slaughter of innocent human beings by other human beings must not be tolerated. The two meaning structures could not be more disparate. Yet both arose from the same murderous death immersion.

Whatever the meaning constructed, it can give rise to an impassioned survivor mission, to which the survivor dedicates much of his or her life. Such a mission is invariably carried out on behalf of the dead. For instance, parents whose children die of leukemia may take on a survivor mission of devoting themselves to research that could cure that disease. Similarly, some Hiroshima survivors have taken on the shared mission of traveling the world to make known everywhere the human effects of nuclear weapons.

The survivor mission is a form of witness. In what one says and does, one is retelling the story of the death encounter, elaborating a new narrative from it. One can be energized by it in ways that contribute to society. But there can be false witness as well. The members of Company C of the Americal Division who would commit the My Lai massacre were already pained survivors, due to deadly ambushes and booby traps as well as a particularly devastating minefield disaster in which 20 percent of the company's men were killed or severely wounded. The night before the slaughter at My Lai, there was a combination "combat briefing" and funeral ceremony (for the dead in general but also for a much admired fatherly sergeant who had met a grotesque death the previous day). Desperate for meaning, the men were exhorted by their officers to find it in "body counts" and to bear witness to their dead buddies by killing "gooks"—in effect, any Vietnamese they encountered.

The American response to 9/11 has a number of motivations, but must be understood in the context of survivor emotions and a survivor mission, as described in the remainder of this chapter. Tragically for us and for the world, much of that response has been a form of false witness. America has mounted a diffuse, Vietnam-style, worldwide "search and destroy mission" on behalf of the 9/11 dead. Here, too, we join the dance with our al–Qaeda "partner," which brings fierce survivor emotions and considerable false witness of its own.

The survivor's quest for meaning can be illuminating and of considerable human value. But it also can be drawn narrowly, manipulatively, and violently, in connection with retribution and pervasive killing.

AMERICAN LEADERS AS SURVIVORS: ANXIETY AND BELLIGERENCE

An important matter for grasping American behavior is the way in which survivor emotions have affected the president and his advisers. I will suggest here only certain observable tendencies.

The president was sitting on a stool in an elementary school classroom in Sarasota, Florida, when told by aides about the first, and then the second, attack on the World Trade Center. Woodward describes a photograph taken at the time that shows Bush's face as having "a distant sober look, almost frozen, edging on bewilderment." While the president later said that he was then thinking about war, there must have been a prior moment of shock and anxiety. Making his first public statement, the president looked "shaken." Certainly an immediate response on the part of people around him—and we must assume, the president himself—was the fear that he might be killed. That included fear for him as a person as well as for the office of the American presidency.

Hence the strange spectacle of the president spending much of the first day, following the early-morning attack, in the air, being flown from Sarasota, Florida, to Shreveport, Louisiana, to Omaha, Nebraska, and finally Washington, DC. His former speechwriter tells us that when Bush spoke to the country from Barksdale Air Force Base in Louisiana, "he looked and sounded like the hunted, not the hunter." At least for that day, the president was clearly on the run. Whatever considerations went into that decision, the fear was not inappropriate: it was plausible that the White House could be attacked. Later information concerning the plane eventually downed in Pennsylvania through the courageous intervention of its passengers suggests that possible targets might have been the White House or the House of Representatives and Senate buildings on Capitol Hill.

What becomes of great importance is one's manner of dealing with death anxiety, and with fear in general. In the case of the president and his advisers, that death anxiety could have contributed greatly to their overall belligerence. The immediate insistence that we were at war had to do not only with the devastating dimensions of the attacks—and with longer-standing projections of American hegemony—but also with the president's own psychological style in relation to anxiety and threat.

Certainly the president and his advisers are by no means alone in responding this way. There is a widespread psychological tendency for people experiencing death anxiety to become aggressive, and in some cases engage in violent rhetoric or actions. When threatened with individual annihilation, one may lash out at others as a means of reasserting one's vitality, of simply *feeling* alive.

Under certain conditions—some forms of military combat, for instance—that response can be useful. But when national leaders respond belligerently, they may tap the collective potential of their people for amorphous rage, which can readily be transformed into war fever. All are better served when the leaders of a superpower acknowledge their anger or rage, while stepping back sufficiently to choose policies that are wise in terms of both national interest and the world in general. This is particularly difficult to do when survivor emotions are raw and accompanied by the superpower's (and its president's) abrupt humiliation.

FAILED ENACTMENT?

Looking at the question of failed enactment and self-condemnation, we may first say that these are unlikely to be emotions the president readily experiences in any conscious way. We have seen that he prides himself on decisiveness, dislikes ambiguity and nuance, and is reinforced in his hyperclarity by his fundamentalist-like religious convictions. He is not a person to reflect—certainly not publicly—on presidential uncertainty or error. Yet 9/11 has confronted him with what could be strongly perceived as failed enactment. The feeling could certainly derive from his and his administration's role in letting 9/11 happen, and possibly also from his immediate reaction to the attacks.

There has been considerable evidence of failure of coordination both among the main intelligence agencies, and between them and the White House. This egregious lack of communication, along with other forms of blundering, resulted in strong evidence of a pending terrorist attack being ignored, including information about some of the actual participants and their intention to hijack planes. There had even been a two-year-old report warning of the possibility of al–Qaeda's crashing planes into government buildings. To be sure, the failure to deal adequately with terrorism extends back at least to the Clinton administration, but 9/11 occurred on the watch of this president. For a military-minded administration, the attack on the Pentagon must have felt particularly humiliating. As one observer has put it, "The Pentagon could not defend the Pentagon."

Like anyone in his position, the president was also vulnerable to a sense of failed enactment at the moment of the attacks, a sense of having been unable to meet his own ideal standards of how a man and a president should behave at that moment. His odd first-day itinerary from Florida to Louisiana to Nebraska was, according to *Time* magazine, disturbing to many. "Some Republicans on the Hill wanted to know why Counsellor Karen Hughes was the highest government official anyone saw on television all day, other than Bush's brief unsettling appearance in Louisiana." Whether or not any related self-critical feelings about his initial lack of a strong national presence entered into Bush's awareness, it would be difficult to escape them altogether. In leaders unable to question themselves or to deviate from moral certainty, such feelings of self-condemnation over failed enactment must be suppressed. One way that can be accomplished is by transforming them into anger and aggressiveness.

In all this, the president clearly experienced a debt to the dead and to surviving family members. During an early visit to Ground Zero he found the scene to be "very, very, very eerie" and the crowd of rescue workers to be "unbelievably emotional" in their demand for justice. While much of the day was scripted, the president was undoubtedly moved by his encounters with victims' families. In that way his scripted words—"America today is on bended knee in prayer for the people whose lives were lost here"—accurately reflected his feelings.

He took on a public role as (in Woodward's words) "mourner in chief" at precisely the time when he and his advisers were making key decisions about the war on terrorism. He was affected by urgent pleas from rescue workers, "Don't let me down." And as the president later recalled: "These people looking at you in the eye, these tired faces, You go get 'em." Bush added, "And we're going to get 'em, there's no question about that." The debt to the dead, and to the immediate survivors representing them, was instantly transformed into a strong impulse toward retaliative action. Such a sequence is hardly unusual, and could be the experience of any national leader. The danger a leader faces is that of equating a sense of debt to the dead with fierce, amorphous retribution.

NUMBING AND FEELING

People who deal regularly with death-related matters undergo what I call *selective professional numbing*. For instance, the surgeon performing an open-heart procedure cannot afford the emotions of the patient's family members. The professional task requires a certain focused detachment. The same is true of political and military leaders who make decisions about violence and war.

But there is a grave danger of excessive professional numbing in the service of what leaders take to be their forceful goals. Such excessive post–9/11 numbing clearly included the blocking out of the potential effects of aggressive American policies on Islamic minds, and the extent to which those policies could increase the terrorist threat to America. It also blocked out significant concern over non-American casualties in either the Afghanistan or the later Iraq war.

The most glaring example of such professional numbing may well have been the very decision to invade Iraq, given its inevitable influence on the resurgence of al–Qaeda and other violent Islamist groups. That terrorist organization, according to *The New York Times*, had been in considerable decline but underwent "a spike in recruitment" and a general resurgence after the invasion began. In that way the numbing experienced by American leaders could later bring about a potential increase in suffering by their own people. Such excessive numbing can prevent any serious consideration of the unintended consequences of violence, whether on those designated as one's enemies or on one's own people.

James Carroll provided an interesting parable for such blunted perception—a fable in which a would-be hero, concerned about chaos among his people, seeks out and subdues a prophetic troll to extract from him the secret of drawing order out of chaos. He is told that for the secret to be revealed, he will have to give the troll his left eye. When he does so, the troll tells him, "The secret of order over chaos is: Watch with both eyes."

Carroll goes on to observe that we embarked on our war with Iraq "with only one eye watching." We saw only Saddam Hussein and the diffuse threat of terrorism he was thought to represent, but did not see the far more deadly reverberations of such a war. These include new forms of chaos in the Middle East, expanded threats of global terrorism, and accelerated nuclear weapons programs in countries which conclude that such weapons might prevent an American invasion. What Carroll calls "our missing eye that makes us blind" is the self-imposed wound of psychic numbing with which we went about this destructive project. That same "missing eye" enabled us to wallow in triumphalism and to see little more than the quick success of our military juggernaut. All this has been part of our larger blindness in pursuing our "war on terrorism."

THE SUSPICIOUS GIANT

The Bush administration had been suspicious toward much of the world long before 9/11. Its sense of superpower prerogative, along with a neoconservative/nationalist hostility toward international institutions and any constraints they might impose on it, were much in evidence in its rejection of treaties placing controls on global warming, on nuclear testing, and on biological weaponry. But 9/11 initiated a process in which that suspiciousness was greatly intensified, became fixed, and has had extraordinary consequences in the world.

One need only look at the remarkable dissipation of the worldwide sympathy for the United States. At the moment of 9/11, the outpouring of goodwill was almost universal: not from only allies and friends in Europe and Asia like Great Britain, Germany, France, Japan, and

South Korea, but from China, Russia, and much of the Middle East. President Mohammad Khatami of Iran expressed "deep regret and sympathy with the victims"; President Bashar al-Assad of Syria was one of the first to denounce the attacks (saying they were as bad as the attacks Israel had carried out against the Palestinians); and President Hosni Mubarak of Egypt called the attacks "horrible and unimaginable," pledging help in tracking down those responsible (though he added that Israel's actions in the Middle East created "an atmosphere that is encouraging terrorism"). Kofi Annan, secretary general of the United Nations, also expressed strong sympathy and suggested that the world organization mount a broadly shared effort at combating world terrorism.

Our decision to reject any such international approach, and choose instead a consistently unilateral war on terrorism, was influenced by survivor suspiciousness toward those who offer help and perception of help as weakness, particularly anathema for a humiliated superpower. The resulting global shift from profound sympathy to fearful antagonism has surely been one of the most far-reaching and dramatic psychological and political turnabouts ever recorded. By early 2003, polls taken in various parts of the world suggested that America was increasingly seen as the most dangerous of all countries. On February 15, 2003, an estimated ten million or more people marched in the streets of 600 cities to protest the forthcoming invasion of Iraq.

This remarkable reversal in world sentiment resulted from our insistent unilateralism. Our aggrieved survivor emotions exacerbated our suspiciousness toward the world in general, magnifying our disinclination toward sharing the earth's problems.

GRANDIOSE MISSION

Most important—and dangerous—has been George W. Bush's sense of being on a survivor mission. He has repeatedly made it clear that September 11 provided him with his life's meaning—as the American president who triumphs over terrorism—and he adopted the war on terrorism as the defining principle of his presidency. The world's most prominent survivor had found his mission.

Prior to 9/11 Bush's presidency was considered lackluster. According to David Frum, the former White House speechwriter, he was devoid of "a big organizing idea" and "was encountering heavy criticism in connection with his economic policies, and was vague about his political vision." He seemed to spend less time working than did most presidents, and to be unable to find a clear personal or public focus.

With 9/11, everything fell into place for him. He became a confident "wartime president." He and his speechwriters were unfortunately accurate in their initial labeling of his approach to terrorism as a "crusade." That word suggests a Christian holy war (deriving as it does from the Latin *crux*, or cross), which is the kind of mission the president seems to have imagined himself on. Of course, the word had to be quickly abandoned because it was too suggestive of the specific Christian holy wars against Muslims, but the idea of a sacred mission became inseparable from his sense of a survivor's debt to the dead and his perceived responsibility to his country and his deity. Given who he was, this survivor mission was inevitably absorbed into the superpower syndrome. Superpower omnipotence became inseparable from "routing out" all terrorists. The survivor mission became cosmic and, like the overall syndrome, immersed in illusion.

This was by no means the only form of survivor mission possible for an American president or the American people. Combating terrorism had to be part of a survivor response, but the task could have been undertaken with greater restraint in the use of force, and with a focus from the very beginning on international cooperation. The survivor mission embarked on by Bush and his advisers strongly affected the meaning structures of Americans in general. While many have drawn more reflective and nuanced meanings from 9/11, there has been little encouragement from above for any deviance from the narrowly grandiose presidential survivor mission.

One must add that President Bush and those around him sometimes waver in their violent transformation of survivor emotions and show signs of stepping back and exercising restraint. Pragmatic pressures affect any presidency, in this case coming from people and nations throughout the world as well as from an ambivalent American public. But when this occurs, these leaders give little indication that the restraint is anything other than a temporary measure. They remain committed to a prior vision of American world dominance, now energized and in their eyes legitimated by their 9/11 survivor mission.

CHAPTER II
STAGES OF RESPONSE

Ordinary Americans derived a wide variety of meanings from 9/11. Many embraced the belligerent survivor mission of their leaders; others sought alternative survivor missions involving a more restrained use of violence and greater emphasis on addressing the causes of terrorism; still others wavered between the two tendencies. A considerable number of people sought personal meaning in the events of 9/11: the importance of devoting oneself more to one's family, a reevaluation of career and accomplishment, or a determination to seek more pleasure in life. But beyond specific survivor meanings, we can identify certain overall American responses. These have occurred in stages, more or less in sequence, with considerable overlap.

VULNERABILITY SHOCK

The first response was the shock of sudden vulnerability.

Not only did most Americans have no warning of 9/11, they had never previously imagined an event of this nature and magnitude (outside perhaps a movie theater)—of hijacked jet planes being intentionally crashed into some of the world's tallest buildings—least of all in their own country, which had never experienced a terrorist act of this dimension or a more traditional invasion by a foreign power since the War of 1812. Undoubtedly, our mindset toward terrorism contained a great deal of denial, given the World Trade Center attack of 1993, the Oklahoma City attack of 1995, and the many signs of militant worldwide opposition to American policies. But it is also true that most Americans had no narrative with which to anticipate, and in that sense psychologically prepare for, what actually took place.

Any death encounter can shatter the preexisting relation between self and world. This one did so abruptly, on a vast scale, and in ways that seemed bizarre to the point of incomprehensibility. The World Trade Center was a preeminent symbol of American financial power, but for people employed in it (or who happened to be nearby), it was also an everyday working area, safe in its ordinariness, until suddenly violated by explosion and fire. In the case of the Pentagon, the brain center and fortress of American military power was itself suddenly made vulnerable. While most Americans were far removed from that direct experience, none could fully avoid a shocking sense of new vulnerability.

The essence of that initial shock was a sudden shift in our perception of the American landscape. What was assumed to be "secure," even impregnable, had become strangely and unpredictably precarious.

Americans have retained these early feelings as a baseline for their sense of terrorist danger. This initial response of shock and vulnerability, ever present, can be reactivated by various forms of threat, and the basic fear it embodies is highly susceptible to manipulation by leaders looked to for protection.

INVISIBLE CONTAMINATION

A second stage of response came with the series of anthrax attacks, through letters containing a refined, weapons-grade form of the bacillus, most occurring only a month or two after 9/11. The letters, sent primarily to Democratic political leaders and media figures, including Senate Majority Leader Tom Daschle and NBC news anchor Tom Brokaw, resulted in twenty-three known cases of anthrax and five deaths. So great was the fear, and the real danger, that all the House and Senate offices were closed. The Hart Senate Office Building remained closed for more than three months; and Senator Daschle's office, which required particularly extensive decontamination, for about five months.

The anthrax letters created a new national sense of emergency. There was a widespread initial perception that the letters were connected to 9/11, especially since they praised Allah and threatened Israel and America. There was a frightening psychological sense that our enemies were capable of doing *anything* to us, including violating an international taboo on biological weapons, a taboo that was both legal (formalized by various international treaties) and psychological (biological weapons are felt to be even more grotesque than nuclear ones), even if that taboo had been violated before by various countries.

The anthrax attacks deepened the American sense of vulnerability, imparting to it the kind of fear of *invisible contamination* that I encountered in Hiroshima survivors in relation to radiation: the fear of a lethal poison, difficult to detect, that might strike one down at any time. Terrorism now seemed capable of penetrating our bodily organs. The situation was further confused by increasing evidence that the source of the anthrax letters was American, that this weapon of mass destruction came from the US Cold War weapons labs, and by published accounts suggesting that the leading suspect was a former government scientist who had worked in our biological weapons program.

Neither that scientist nor anyone else has been officially accused of the attacks, and possibly because their origins were apparently American, not Middle Eastern, the anthrax attacks have seldom been mentioned by the Bush administration and have diminished in public awareness. While there was some relief in discovering that the 9/11 foreign perpetrators did not seem to be responsible,

Americans were confronted with the no less troubling thought of anthrax-related danger from within.

TIMELESS DREAD

A third stage of response has been the fear of terrorism rendered chronic. This has taken the form of a pervasive, timeless dread, the feeling that we can never be free of this ominous threat, that we may be awaiting a moment that could dwarf 9/11. It has become increasingly difficult to envision a future free of that dread. This sense of *futurelessness* came to resemble the experience many had during the Cold War in relation to the superpower nuclear threat. People began to talk, as they had during the Cold War, of emigrating to a safer place such as Australia or New Zealand, or in the case of New Yorkers simply of leaving the city.

This fear of futurelessness has to do with a break in the flow of generations, an interruption of human continuity. While we may be conscious of such a break or interruption only periodically, the anxiety it instills in us becomes associated with a threat to collective existence.

DOUBTS AND RESENTMENTS

A fourth stage arrived with the buildup of doubts and resentments about the directions our leaders' mission has taken us in. These emotions surfaced in the period leading up to the war in Iraq, were suppressed as the war took place, and at the time of this writing are once again strongly reasserting themselves. Such doubts both reflect and further feed prevailing anxieties. Individual people vary greatly in how they experience and express their doubts, but no one can remain completely free of them. As war fever over Iraq waned in the postwar months, questions about the effectiveness of American policies were bound to be aired. With suspicions that our aggressive "war on terrorism" was increasing the dangers we faced and that our quick war to "disarm" Saddam Hussein may have led us into an endless struggle in the Middle East, public doubts increased about whether, so many months after September 11, we are any better prepared for terrorist attacks.

These doubts have been reinforced by at least two authoritative studies, one by former Senators Gary Hart and Warren Rudman for the Council on Foreign Relations, and another sponsored by Congress, both of which found considerable fault with the domestic security measures we have taken. The problem is inherently excruciating as everyone (even when part of a superpower) struggles with the realization that there is no such thing as complete freedom from terrorist danger. But the administration's sudden dire warnings of imminent attack and its erratic approach to domestic security—from color-coded warnings to ill-conceived programs to administer smallpox vaccine, from recommendations of duct tape to overblown accounts of foiled terrorist plots—have done little to allay American doubts and fears and much to increase them. The administration's manipulation of fear, always with the promise of ultimate protection, can work for a certain period of time, but the fear will not go away.

THE WAR ON IRAQ

With the attack on Iraq the administration at first seemed successful in overcoming opposition and unease. But if war fever can relieve doubts for some, at least temporarily, it almost immediately intensifies them for others. During the buildup to the war, there were widely expressed fears not only that the war would cause an increase in terrorism, but that its "preventive" rationale would lead quickly to more such wars—and there was an accompanying suspicion that in its timing it was meant to rally the country behind the patriotic "war on terrorism," and behind the president's reelection. Robert Byrd, the senior statesman of the Senate, had that kind of numbed patriotism in mind when he spoke of the country as "sleepwalking through history."

Significantly, some months earlier the administration had already convinced a slight majority of American "sleepwalkers" that it could better protect them than could the opposition party, and so won a marginal yet important victory in the 2002 congressional elections. It did so by honing in on the issue of patriotism while making considerable political capital out of its orchestration of existing fear. But the enormous number of Americans uniquely engaged in protest demonstrations before a war even began suggested the depths of seething resentment in a profoundly divided nation. The protesters questioned the motivations behind the war, the administration's high-handed unilateral and preemptive policies, and the numbed patriotism of the rest of the American population.

The actual invasion of Iraq abruptly changed the American psychic landscape. While there were extensive protests right up to, and after, the moment of invasion, the country at large quickly rallied around the flag and the commander in chief, with high approval ratings for both the war and the president. Americans were mesmerized by the "shock and awe" Baghdad bombing spectacle that began the war, including its display of video-game-like high-tech accuracy, sometimes accompanied by scenes of visual beauty (explosions under a waning moon). But there remained considerable uneasiness about this demonstration of unlimited and unopposed American power. Americans could thrill to the brilliant success of the ground war and to seemingly complete victory after less than three weeks of fighting, but could also wonder why it had all been so easy, and in some cases become troubled by evidence of extensive Iraqi casualties. Most Americans responded, according to public opinion polls, as they were meant to, with celebratory enthusiasm for a noble victory, while a significant minority saw the world's most powerful military machine decimating a small, weak country and were ashamed.

Americans were particularly confused by the responses of Iraqis. There were no flowers-in-hand receptions of the kind predicted by some American leaders. There was some fierce but very brief military resistance. There were early scenes of apparent joy on the part of the populace, featuring the dramatic toppling and smashing (with considerable help from US marine tanks) of the most gigantic of all the Saddam Hussein statues. That image of the tumbling, disintegrating statue was seized upon by American cable-television networks, replayed endlessly, and applauded by the president as emblematic of the administration claim that it had embarked on a war of liberation which would free Iraqis from the control of a murderous dictator. But it later turned out that only a couple of hundred Iraqis actually took part in the demonstration. And while many Iraqis initially seemed to feel great relief that Saddam had gone, the mood would darken, revealing within a matter of days that American planners had prepared well for war but not for "peace." Our military units could not in the ensuing months even restore electric power in the capital to the levels maintained by the previous regime, no less provide jobs for a largely unemployed people and a demoblized Iraqi army.

THE "END" OF THE WAR

Subsequent events gave Americans still more pause. They did not know quite what to make of the extreme chaos and extraordinary destructiveness Iraqis exhibited: of the fires set in the buildings of most former ministries in Baghdad, and the extraordinary looting of everything from hospital gurneys to cultural artifacts from the National Museum of Antiquities and manuscripts from the National Library, treasures that dated back to the beginnings of human civilizations and the origins of Mesopotamian culture.

There were also signs of early political power struggles, including the murder of a prominent Shiite cleric sponsored by the British and Americans, apparently by a rival group; large-scale protest demonstrations by Islamic groups, mainly Shiite but also Sunni, denouncing Saddam Hussein but increasingly antagonistic to the American "occupiers," demanding that they leave quickly so that Iraq could be governed by Islamics; and finally the emergence of what occupying military authorities have reluctantly admitted is a low-level but deadly guerilla warfare against American and British forces as well as the Iraqis aiding them. If Americans have been puzzled by this postwar chaos, they have been even more so by Iraqis' angry blaming of the occupiers for it. So extreme was the situation that the Americans appointed to administer the country were quickly replaced, while in Baghdad and in the Sunni parts of the country the ongoing guerrilla war began to result in a growing number of American casualties.

American deaths have been relatively small in number,

about 278 at this writing, approximately one-half of which have resulted from attacks on occupying soldiers after the president declared the war over and victory ours. During the war the recording of these deaths had been accompanied by extensive media glorification of heroic American behavior under fire and especially on the part of rescued American POW Private Jessica Lynch. All this, largely government-sponsored, was aimed at encouraging a national survivor mission of affirming the noble military project of the "fallen" men and women, and reasserting support for this war and others to follow if necessary.

That was the president's message in his grandly if duplicitously staged victory speech on the USS *Abraham Lincoln* aircraft carrier. (He was flown in by fighter plane and was even said to have briefly taken the controls, after the carrier had been elaborately diverted from San Diego so that he could descend histrionically from the clouds rather than walk more prosaically up a ramp.) Undoubtedly many Americans were drawn to this image of their superpower president as a "top-gun" military hero; others were appalled by what they saw as a disturbing form of hollow triumphalism that reflected a superpower's increasing militarization.

The returns from America's Iraqi military project are far from in, including public response to continuing "postwar" casualties and the likelihood that more than 100,000 American troops may be destined to occupy Iraq indefinitely at a cost that will further strain the shaky American economy. There remains the possibility, over time, of an opposite survivor reaction taking hold, especially if casualties continue to mount from resistance to the occupation, or from wars with other Middle Eastern countries. Doubts could build about the cause for which Americans died—about Iraq's elusive weapons of mass destruction and the credibility of our leaders in declaring their existence as a threat to the United States, about what the Iraq war and 9/11 actually had to do with each other, even about the deaths of large numbers of Iraqis and possibly others in the area—all of which could lead to a survivor mission of stopping the killing. That was the kind of psychological process that helped end the Vietnam war.

Finally, Americans must struggle with another contradiction that lies at the heart of our mission in the Middle East, concerning our future interaction with the Islamic world. On the one hand, many respond to the administration's military ethos, including support for its threats to Iran and Syria, and even for possible invasions to bring about "regime change" in either or both of those countries. On the other hand, deepening chaos in Iraq and elsewhere in the Middle East may stir strong fears of engaging in continuous wars in that area—or elsewhere such as North Korea—and of renewed terrorism in the United States as a consequence. For both Americans who rally behind their president and those who strongly oppose his policies, there has to be considerable trepidation about their own and their country's future, and that of the world as well.

THE DOUBLE LIFE

Most Americans have adapted to the threat of 9/11 in the manner they did to nuclear fear: that is, by resorting to a kind of double life. They go about their routines, their jobs, and family involvements in their usual ways, while in another part of the self they are aware that, in a moment and without warning, they and everything and everyone around them could be annihilated. This limited, everyday dissociation permits us all to carry on reasonably effectively in our lives. But it cannot fully overcome lingering anxiety, which may be painfully activated by events or images, nearby or far away, associated in people's minds with terrorism. The depth of this fear and the ease with which it may reassert itself leaves Americans open to significant emotional manipulation by leaders all too ready to enlist them in an apocalyptic superpower mission that they might otherwise call into question, even strongly oppose. Such primal experiences of fear prepare people to resonate to the persistent drumbeat of the administration's "war on terrorism."

American psyches can be further strained by the erratic leadership to which they are often subjected. Effective leadership in any crisis requires a balance of candor and hope. This administration, at its worst, has wavered between excessive secrecy and sudden, dire warnings of the "inevitability" of terrorist attacks with weapons of mass destruction on our soil—warnings that often seem to be timed to deflect embarrassing criticism about official measures taken to prevent or prepare for terrorism. On other occasions, the administration has spoken in more even tones. But there remains much uncertainty about the connection between what the administration says and what it does about terrorism, and the relationship of these words and actions to the dangers Americans perceive themselves to face.

Americans therefore have been left with a mixture of enthusiasm, confusion, anxiety, and anger in relation to the official survivor mission their government has embraced in their name following upon 9/11. And there is lingering unease about our targeted but still unaccounted for demons, Osama bin Laden, Mullah Omar, and Saddam Hussein, who in one way or another, dead or alive, continue to haunt us.

CHAPTER 12
FLUID WORLD CONTROL

The invasion of Iraq was a continuation of the American military apocalyptic: of destroying what is deemed necessary for the reshaping of a designated part of the world. The extremity of the project and the utopian dreams of global domination that lay beneath it were hidden behind administration assertions about the need for disarmament, regime change, and democratization. Inevitably, the war-fighting, which was the destructive phase, was much more efficient than what columnist William P. Pfaff called the "planned (or as it seems, largely unplanned) pacification and reconstruction" of Iraq that followed. But as he went on to say, "The moment of victory has been seized to start reshaping the Middle East." This attempted reshaping of the whole region according to an American world vision has already involved strong pressures on Syria, Lebanon, and Iran, aimed minimally at intimidation and the curbing of possible terrorist or simply unfriendly activities, and maximally at regime change, possibly through invasion. It has also involved setting up a string of bases in areas formerly controlled by the Soviet Union in Central Asia as well as Eastern Europe.

Included as well is a policy of "strip[ping] from the United Nations its political functions," so that there will be no future international restraints on American power. Instead the Bush administration seeks "democratic coalitions" under its own control in every region, thereby creating "a world run by the United States, backed by as many states as will sign on to support it." Hence the invasion of Iraq, as Jay Bookman, columnist for the *Atlanta Journal-Constitution* put it, was "intended to mark the official emergence of the United States as a full-fledged global empire, seizing sole responsibility and authority as planetary policeman."

THE OWNERSHIP OF HISTORY

But this "global empire" does not follow previous imperial models, say, of the British empire from the eighteenth to the twentieth century. There is no American plan for leaving elaborate bureaucracies in every country we dominate. While all previous empires claimed some kind of noble mission, the new American mission contains a particularly fervent rendering of Wilsonian altruism. The National Security Strategy statement that the administration released in September 2002 speaks grandly of the American intention "to extend the benefits of freedom across the globe" and "to help make the world not just safer but better."

At the same time it makes clear that, into the foreseeable future, America intends to hold absolute military dominance—one might say omnipotence—on our planet: "The United States," as the National Security Strategy puts it, "must and will maintain the capability to defeat any attempt by an enemy—whether state or non-state actor—to impose its will on the United States, our allies, or our friends. We will maintain the forces sufficient to support our obligations, and to defend freedom. Our forces will be strong enough to dissuade potential adversaries from pursuing a military buildup in hopes of surpassing, or equaling, the power of the United States." Bookman concurs with many observers in describing this strategy as "a plan for permanent US military and economic domination of every region of the globe."

The Bush administration's projection of American power extends not only over planet Earth, but through the militarization of space, over the heavens as well. Its strategists dream of deciding the outcome of significant world events everywhere. We may call this an empire of *fluid world control*, and theirs is nothing less than an inclusive claim to the *ownership of history*. It is a claim never made before because never before has technology permitted the imagining of such an enterprise, however illusory, on the part of a head of state and his inner circle.

The administration's strategic document quotes a phrase from one of the president's speeches concerning the dangers we face "at the crossroads of radicalism and technology." What is meant by that phrase is the apocalyptic marriage between ultimate zealotry and ultimate weapons in our enemies, but the "crossroads" mentioned applies no less to American policy, specifically as laid out in this document. The administration's radicalism takes the form of aggressively remaking the world in an American image. Our unprecedented world dominance, made possible by our unique military technology, becomes our means of doing so. The fluidity of this version of imagined world control is consistent with the Rumsfeld doctrine of a fluid military. The latter is to sustain the former. Technology and fluidity are counted upon to minimize American casualties and streamline war-making in general. (American leaders for instance claimed the victory in Iraq demonstrates that, to win wars, we no longer have to engage in saturation bombing of cities as in World War II.)

These policies have recently been attributed to the influence of a conservative German-born University of Chicago political philosopher Leo Strauss on a number of leading neoconservatives in the administration. Strauss has been understood by some to have advocated various forms of governmental elitism and authoritarianism, but whatever influence he might have had on American policy zealots like Paul Wolfowitz, I would stress the newness and highly contemporary nature of American efforts at world control. Strauss, who believed in the wisdom of classical Greek thinkers, could hardly have imagined either the extremity of American military dominance or the equally extraordinary international communications technology now available. All this makes the current American mission *sui generis*, one that has no precedent and is creating itself as it proceeds.

The National Security Strategy put forward a unique doctrine of preventive strikes or wars against terrorists or other potential enemies, as well as unilateral action wherever American interests are at stake: "While the United States will constantly strive to enlist the support of the international community, we will not hesitate to act alone, if necessary . . ." The document not only lacks any principle of restraint on American power or American control—which is itself of the greatest psychological importance—but insists that there be no such restraint. And all is justified, the document states, quoting the president, by an American determination "to answer these attacks [of 9/11] and rid the world of evil."

The National Security Strategy is in fact a statement of American susceptibility to the lure of the infinite—to a vision of achieving total sway over human endeavors. It represents a kind of omega point of superpower omnipotence and megalomania.

This claim on infinity inevitably turns Orwellian, as James Carroll warns: "Defense becomes offense, the protection of your children becomes the murder of another's, his threat becomes your preemption. You kill to stop the killing. Then you wonder, Are you the victim, or the slayer? But you are both."

Yet a sense of megalomania and omnipotence, whether in an individual or a superpower, must sooner or later lead not to glory but collapse. The ownership of history is a fantasy in the extreme. Infinite power and control is a temptation that is as self-destructive as it is dazzling—still another version of the ownership of death.

THE HAUNTED SUPERPOWER

The world's only superpower is haunted by a fear of weakness. From psychiatric experience with individuals, we know that underneath expressions of megalomania and claims to omnipotence there tend to be profound feelings of powerlessness and emptiness. Feelings on that order may affect our leaders' projections of world control. These could take the form of fear of the political fragmentation of our society, with accompanying death anxiety related not just to 9/11 but to the potential collapse of the superpower entity itself. Underneath our leaders' arrogant certainties concerning the world, there may lie profound doubts about our own social and national integration, about America's control of itself. Fear of being out of control can lead to the most aggressive efforts at total control of everyone else.

Helping to overcome such fear is the claim to transcendent American virtue, to providing beneficent and liberating service to the world. That sense of a mission both altruistic and sacred can generate a surge of power that, in turn, suppresses feelings of powerlessness and weakness.

Fear of weakness is, of course, bound up with related feelings of vulnerability, with a superpower's sense of being a very visible target, and with its unrealizable requirement of omnipotence. The world's only superpower has become a target not just because it is so dominant but because its recent policies and attitudes, emerging from superpower syndrome, have antagonized just about everyone. Its unrealizable omnipotence has caused its leaders to embark on an aggressive quest for absolute security via domination, which is another form of entrapment in infinity.

Former Secretary of State Henry Kissinger, coming out in support of the Bush administration, made a case for invading Iraq based on a principle of "ultimate national security." But as the political scientist David C. Hendrickson pointed out at the time, Kissinger seemed to have forgotten his own earlier criticism of the "absolute security" sought by revolutionary powers, noting then that "the desire of one power for absolute security means absolute insecurity for all the others." In this sense and in the way that the present administration has sought to overthrow world diplomatic procedures and restraints on war-making, the United States has certainly become a "revolutionary power" in pursuit of absolute security and absolute invulnerability. But the fear of weakness will not go away.

IRAQ AND WORLD CONTROL

Consider again the invasion of Iraq. Three reasons, given varied emphasis at different times, were put forward to justify the American war: the disarmament of Iraq in connection with its reputed stockpiles of weapons of mass destruction in violation of United Nations resolutions; the need for "regime change" to remove an evil dictator; and the opportunity to make Iraq into a democracy and thereby begin to democratize the Middle East. A fourth reason, publicly emphasized only by opponents of the war, was a lust for the control of Iraqi oil, which represents a significant part of the industrial world's future oil supplies. I believe that each of these four motivations mattered, not in itself but as part of a larger superpower impulse toward world control.

Insistence upon disarmament, for instance, had to do with an American intolerance for potentially unfriendly countries possessing or even desiring to possess weapons of mass destruction, whatever the uncertainty of their existence in Iraq. As of July 2003, two months after the subjugation of that country, American military inspection teams had found no biological or chemical weapons in Iraq, or any evidence that Iraq had had even the most basic elements of a nuclear program in place before the war. From the beginning, Bush administration statements and presentations have exaggerated, distorted, and sometimes falsified evidence in order to make the claim that weapons of mass destruction existed, and that such weapons endangered the national security of the United States. Within the paradoxical political psychology involved, Iraq's elusive weapons of mass destruction were both a fabricated excuse for invasion and a genuine source of anxiety as a potential threat to American *absolute* security.

"Regime change" had to do not so much with simply removing a murderous dictator from power (over the years we had supported or tolerated Saddam Hussein at the height of his cruelty, even when he launched poison-gas attacks on Iran and on his own people) but with removing leadership hostile to us, which touched the raw nerve of superpower vulnerability.

The vision of remaking Iraq and the entire Middle East in our democratic image, part of a grandiose dream of transforming the world, on the other hand, reflected a sense of superpower omnipotence. American invaders did find extensive evidence of torture and mass killing by the regime, which, while hardly a surprise, enabled us to mobilize our claimed altruism in the service of a broader project of controlling history.

Even a desire for Iraq's enormous oil reserves, the most concrete and venal of the motivations for invasion, should be seen as subsumed to larger regional and global plans to which control of such energy reserves would surely contribute. The Bush administration did not make war on Iraq simply for the oil, but for control of a strategic land and its resources in order to carry out its visionary world project.

Radical (though usually called "neoconservative") American geopolitical strategists had targeted Iraq, at least since the early 1990s, as a key to American hegemony in the Middle East. In their projection, oil, disarmament, regime change, and the spread of American-style democracy were all part of sustaining an ever-threatened sense of superpower invulnerability. All four motivations were subsumed to the ownership of history. There are always elements of mystery in an apocalyptic quest (even to those who most actively promote it), but in this case there is no mystery about the superpower syndrome at its core.

NUCLEAR CONTRADICTIONS

Nuclear weapons represent a psychological ground zero for the contradictions of the syndrome. The syndrome demands absolute nuclear dominance and equally absolute security in relation to weapons possessors throughout the world. This security "requirement" means we are to determine who may possess nuclear weapons and who may not. But the United States has little actual control over whether such weapons enter others' hands, and has even more difficulty controlling attitudes toward the weapons. With Iraq we settled the matter militarily, knowing that it had no nuclear weapons, and discovered that it had no nuclear program either. With North Korea our blustering approach and threats of military intervention actually seem to have spurred that country to produce a few of the weapons even more quickly.

It must be said that any such proliferation is dangerous to the world and hard to stop. But superpower syndrome propels us toward desperately belligerent solutions that only worsen the problem, as opposed to genuine diplomacy, which would include greater restraint in our own nuclear policies and significant reductions in our stockpiles, not to mention participation in a longer-term attempt to rid the world, ourselves included, of such apocalyptic weaponry. Out of fear of weakness and vulnerability, the superpower calls forth its military activism to reassert its claim to omnipotence. In the name of "counter-proliferation" measures, proliferation is psychologically stimulated.

At the same time, our leaders have exploited the nuclear fear of Americans for geopolitical and military purposes. The Gulf War of 1990–91 gained congressional support only after George Bush Sr. declared that there was new evidence about the advanced nature of Iraq's nuclear project. More recently, the younger Bush's administration, in attempting to demonstrate Saddam Hussein's active pursuit of a nuclear weapons program, did not just provide dubious or misleading evidence (as in the case of a number of other claims, such as Saddam's alleged ties to al–Qaeda), it made use of completely forged and falsified documents, no doubt originated by others but passed on by our own intelligence agencies under pressure to support the American argument. The temptation of our leaders is to tap into primal American nuclear fear in order to affirm their own aggressive fear-driven policies.

Nuclear fear comes to be juxtaposed with fear of terrorism, and the combination is politically manipulated in the direction of military solutions to be carried out by those in power; their message is that only military might can protect us. In that way nuclear fear becomes a key lever for the militarization of society.

NUCLEAR FEAR AND NUMBING

There have been various shifts in the intensity of nuclear fear over recent decades. During the 1980s, studies showed that many Americans, children and adults, did not expect to be able to live out their lives because they believed some form of nuclear holocaust was coming. One could say that such fear was appropriate to the danger inherent in a world dominated by two hostile, nuclear-armed superpowers, and that it contributed a certain amount of energy to efforts on the part of a burgeoning antinuclear movement to remove or diminish that danger.

During the 1990s, nuclear fear demonstrably decreased, in part replaced by fears of environmental catastrophe and of global pandemics like AIDS, but a larger influence was undoubtedly an increase in psychic numbing associated with the assumption that the end of the Cold War meant the end of nuclear danger. Actually, long-term nuclear danger may have increased because of "trickle-down nuclearism" and related tendencies toward accelerated proliferation, and also because of the large number of unaccounted for or poorly guarded weapons and nuclear materials in the former Soviet republics and Russia. The absence of nuclear fear, then, meant that we lacked appropriate feelings about the actual threat we faced. Unfortunately, that psychological dysfunction contributed greatly to the American failure to take advantage of a unique post–Cold War opportunity for radical worldwide denuclearization.

By the turn of the millennium, India and Pakistan were involved in aggressively escalating nuclear testing programs while facing each other across a heavily armed frontier—a signal that we were entering the second nuclear age. While it is early to gauge twentieth-first-century nuclear fear, a particular pattern seems to be emerging for Americans. Under the influence of nuclearistic leaders eager to make such weapons part of their war plans, we have acquiesced in our own second nuclear age, with little note of the massive suffering and dying that could result. At the height of nuclear awareness (and nuclear fear) during the early 1980s, there was a widespread realization that the use of such weaponry would be catastrophic for *everyone*—for the United States, the Soviet Union, and the rest of the world. But in anticipating our own more "creative" use of smaller weapons, there is an unstated assumption that they will not be all that harmful—just efficient for specific military purposes. The pattern here is one of numbing toward the human effects of one's own nuclear weapons, along with intense, fearful awareness of the grotesque dangers of the weapons of others—for instance, those of North Korea.

"*OUR* WEAPONS ARE GOOD"

All this has a history. When I was working in Hiroshima in 1962, there were various antinuclear movements among the Japanese, each with its position about nuclear weapons. There was a pro-Soviet movement that said, "American nuclear weapons and Chinese nuclear weapons are weapons of war, while Russian nuclear weapons are weapons of peace." There was a pro-Chinese movement that said, "American and Soviet nuclear weapons are weapons of war, while Chinese nuclear weapons are weapons of peace." And there were pro-American voices saying, "Chinese and Russian nuclear weapons are weapons of war, while American nuclear weapons are weapons of peace." These claims could be nothing but painful absurdities for most of the people of Hiroshima, who had the simple idea that all nuclear weapons were cruel and inhuman.

Thus, when the leaders of the only superpower speak of their option to use nuclear weapons, they seize upon the general psychological pattern in which "*our* weapons are good but *theirs* are bad." We may call this *psychic numbing toward one's own weapons*. The assumption is that nobody need be afraid of them because they will be used only for good purposes and will not really hurt people, except perhaps for a few bad guys. *Their* weapons, on the other hand, are nasty and dangerous, and must not be permitted to exist. Such numbing is by no means absolute and can be penetrated from time to time by awareness of weapons truths. But there is a persistent tendency to lapse into this nuclear dichotomy.

At issue is a double illusion: that one's own nuclear weapons are ethically superior to those of others, and that they will be manageable in their use and beneficent in their effects. Embracing that double illusion, the American superpower becomes especially menacing because of its nuclear dominance, its impulse toward use, and its quest for world control. All of these nuclear contradictions are closely bound up with superpower syndrome. They derive from it and also exacerbate it.

SUPERPOWER SYNDROME

In speaking of *superpower syndrome*, I mean to suggest a harmful disorder. I use this medical association to convey psychological and political *abnormality*. I also wish to emphasize a *confluence* of behavior patterns: in any syndrome there is not just a single tendency but a constellation of tendencies. Though each can be identified separately, they are best understood as manifestations of an overarching dynamic that controls the behavior of the larger system, in this case the American national entity.

The dynamic takes shape around a bizarre American collective mindset that extends our very real military power into a fantasy of cosmic control, a mindset all too readily tempted by an apocalyptic mission. The symptoms are of a piece, each consistent with the larger syndrome: unilateralism in all-important decisions, including those relating to war-making; the use of high technology to secure the ownership of death and of history; a sense of entitlement concerning the right to identify and destroy all those considered to be terrorists or friends of terrorists, while spreading "freedom" and virtues seen as preeminently ours throughout the world; the right to decide who may possess weapons of mass destruction and who may not, and to take military action, using nuclear weapons if necessary, against any nation that has them or is thought to be manufacturing them; and underlying these symptoms, a righteous vision of ridding the world of evil and purifying it spiritually and politically.

We are talking about a serious syndrome, one that is profoundly harmful, even fatal, to the national body it inhabits as well as to the world in which that body lives. Yet the syndrome can be countered—if not "cured," at least modified, altered, eventually overcome.

CHAPTER 13
STEPPING OUT OF THE SYNDROME

We can do better. America is capable of wiser, more measured approaches, more humane applications of our considerable power and influence in the world. These may not be as far away as they now seem, and can be made closer by bringing our imaginations to bear on them. Change must be political, of course, but certain psychological contours seem necessary to it.

As a start, we do not have to collude in partitioning the world into two contending apocalyptic forces. We are capable instead of reclaiming our moral compass, of finding further balance in our national behavior. So intensely have we embraced superpower syndrome that emerging from it is not an easy task. Yet in doing so we would relieve ourselves of a burden of our own creation—the psychic burden of insistent illusion. For there is no greater weight than that one takes on when pursuing total power.

We need to draw a new and different lesson from Lord Acton's nineteenth-century assertion: "Power tends to corrupt and absolute power corrupts absolutely." Acton was not quite right. The corruption begins not with the acquisition of power but with the *quest* for and *claim* to absolute power. Ever susceptible to the seductive promise that twenty-first-century technology can achieve world control, the superpower can best resist that temptation by recognizing the corruption connected with that illusion.

STEPPING OFF THE TREADMILL

To renounce the claim to total power would bring relief not only to everyone else, but, soon enough, to citizens of the superpower itself. For to live out superpower syndrome is to place oneself on a treadmill that eventually has to break down. In its efforts to rule the world and to determine history, the United States is, in actuality, working against itself, subjecting itself to constant failure. It becomes a Sisyphus with bombs, able to set off explosions but unable to cope with its own burden, unable to roll its heavy stone to the top of the hill in Hades. Perhaps the crucial step in ridding ourselves of superpower syndrome is recognizing that history cannot be controlled, fluidly or otherwise.

Stepping off the superpower treadmill would also enable us to cease being a nation ruled by fear.

Renouncing omnipotence might make our leaders—or at least future leaders—themselves less fearful of weakness, and diminish their inclination to instill fear in their people as a means of enlisting them for military efforts at illusory world hegemony. Without the need for invulnerability, everyone would have much less to be afraid of.

What we call the historical process is largely unpredictable, never completely manageable. All the more so at a time of radical questioning of the phenomenon of nationalism and its nineteenth- and twentieth-century excesses. In addition, there has been a general decline in confidence in the nation state, and in its ability to protect its people from larger world problems such as global warming or weapons of mass destruction. The quick but dangerous substitute is the superpower, which seeks to fill the void with a globalized, militarized extension of American nationalism. The traditional nation state, whatever its shortcomings, could at least claim to be grounded in a specific geographic area and a particular people or combination of peoples. The superpower claims to "represent" everyone on earth, but it lacks legitimacy in the eyes of those it seeks to dominate, while its leaders must struggle to mask or suppress their own doubts about any such legitimacy.

The American superpower is an artificial construct, widely perceived as illegitimate, whatever the acquiescence it coerces in others. Its reign is therefore inherently unstable. Indeed, its reach for full-scale world domination marks the beginning of its decline. A large task for the world, and for Americans in particular, is the early recognition and humane management of that decline.

HOPE AND IMAGINATION

I write this book in a spirit of hope. Hope is always bound up with the reach of our imagination. We have the capacity to probe painful truths in connection with all apocalyptic violence, and to make contact with the human suffering involved. With such imaginative acts, we begin to take small steps in alternative directions. That conviction has been part of all of my work on twentieth-century excess.

Here I think of an experience I had in the early stages of my study of Nazi doctors. After my first set of interviews in Germany, I went to see a friend of mine, an Auschwitz survivor who was keenly interested in the work. As we sat over coffee, I said to him in a tone that was not without a bit of self-pity: "I appreciate your encouragement, but the truth is that I've begun to have terrible dreams. In my dreams I'm behind barbed wire in some kind of a camp. Worse than that, my wife, and at times my two children, are there in the camp with me." My friend looked directly at me and answered in a matter-of-fact tone that was neither unkind nor especially sympathetic, "Good, now you can do the study." He was telling me that unless I took in some small part of the pain of the victims, the work would have little significance.

Over time, that conversation took on broader meaning for me. We need to bear witness, compassionately, to the destructive events of our era if we are to embark on a more humane course. In that sense the researcher's task extends ever outward. It is not that any study or set of observations can themselves bring about measurable change. Rather, such imaginative efforts enter into the confusions and possibilities of collective consciousness. My belief is that it takes a certain amount of critical and empathic energy from many directions to enable any society to begin to chart a wiser course. This is painfully true of our responses to large-scale killing and dying and our attempts to interrupt that process. All this was implicit in that little conversation with my friend.

Such empathic imagination is all the more necessary when one considers a kind of psychological injustice that can occur in connection with the experiences of victims and perpetrators. I have mentioned survivors' susceptibility to paradoxical guilt, forms of self-condemnation they by no means deserve—together with a full array of painful survivor feelings. In contrast, those responsible for vast killing and dying—for the Nazi genocide or the Hiroshima and Nagasaki bombings—may experience little or no self-condemnation, or obvious psychological pain of any kind. They may be decision-makers, quite removed from any visceral sense of the consequences of their decisions, and even if they are more directly involved in the killing, their technology (gas chambers or high-altitude bombing runs) can render their numbing mechanisms quite effective. Perpetrators thus enlist forms of dissociation which enable them to do what they do. For zealots, the numbing and dissociation can be as extreme as their ideology, particularly when the pursuit of their sacred mission comes to virtually fill their perceptions.

That is why grasping any destructive historical action requires one to examine both ends of the slaughter. One needs to look at the psychological experience of both Auschwitz survivors and Nazi perpetrators; of both Hiroshima survivors and atomic-bomb decision-makers; of both victims of the 9/11 disaster and Islamist terrorists; of both Iraqi civilians and American war planners. One cannot understand the nature of the perpetrators' psychic numbing without studying the full ordeal of their victims. Only then can one gain a fuller grasp of the killing and apply that knowledge toward heading off newer versions of it.

BEYOND VICTIMIZATION

Yet victimization, too, can be absolutized in dangerous ways. Hiroshima leaders over the years have told me about struggles among survivors to overcome exaggerated forms of what they called "victim consciousness." By that they meant an exclusive or totalized focus on their victimization. This could include seeing themselves as the most significant of all victims, or even as the only *true* victims.

As a result, I was told, some could find little other focus in life and feel themselves forever frustrated by insufficient recognition of their victimization. One way that some Hiroshima survivors sought to overcome this pattern was to arrange meetings with Holocaust survivors, in which they exchanged experiences and ideas for combating large-scale killing. Totalized victimization, they found, was best countered by empathy for others who, like themselves, had suffered greatly.

That danger of totalized victim consciousness looms large in connection with 9/11. America was attacked. More than 3,000 people were murdered, whether at the World Trade Center, the Pentagon, or in crashed airplanes. In response, fierce feelings of victimization have been poured into unrestrained but narrowly conceived survivor missions. For a superpower in particular, the mindset of victimization can readily be seized upon and turned into a sense of unlimited entitlement. Justification is then felt in drawing from a broad repertoire of violence to reassert a sense of hegemony, of control over world events, and the need to do so can become so great that an enemy is required.

Significantly, there is a parallel mindset of victimization among Islamist terrorists. They see Islam as having been victimized historically by the West, as well as by its own despotic leaders, and they see themselves and their coreligionists undergoing continuing victimization by the United States.

In both cases, victimization by others becomes the persistent leitmotif, a continuous source of motivation for eliminating the evil forces responsible for that humiliation, and by means that readily extend to apocalyptic purification.

In this vicious circle of victimization and violence, superpower syndrome looms large. For just as a superpower extends its sense of potency into omnipotence, so is it inclined to extend its sense of victimization into total, abject violation. Yet a superpower is also in a unique position to interrupt this dangerous psychological interaction. Its extraordinary power can permit restraint. The irony is that to call forth such restraint, to curb its aggressive message of victimization, it must cease to be a superpower, at least in its omnipotent form. For omnipotence and totalized victim-consciousness are of a piece. They can be jettisoned together by a superpower beginning to emerge from its own syndrome.

AMBIGUITY AND MORTALITY

Stepping out of that syndrome would also include surrendering the claim of certainty, of ownership of truth and reality. That ownership gives rise to deadly righteousness, with a claim to illumination so absolute as to transcend ordinary restraints against mass violence. The healthier alternative is an acceptance of some measure of ambiguity, of inevitable elements of confusion and contradiction, whether in relation to large historical events or in matters of personal experience. This would include a more nuanced approach to Islam and Islamist thought and behavior that allows for the possibility of evolution and change.

It is often claimed that no such acceptance of ambiguity is possible because superpowers, like nations, like people, are uncomfortable with it, that the tendency is always to seek clarity and something close to certainty. But this assumption may well underestimate our psychological capabilities. Ambiguity, in fact, is central to human function, recognized and provided for by cultural institutions and practices everywhere. American society in particular has cultivated the kinds of ambiguity that go with multiplicity and with shifting populations and frontiers.

I have tried in my past work to formulate a version of the self as many-sided, flexible, and capable of change and transformation. This *protean self* (named after Proteus, the Greek sea god who was capable of taking on many shapes) stands in direct contrast to the fundamentalist or apocalyptic self. Indeed, the closed fundamentalist self and its apocalyptic impulses can be understood as a reaction to protean tendencies, which are widely abroad in our world as a response to the complexities of recent history. Any contemporary claim to absolute certainty, then, is compensatory, an artificial plunge into totalism that seeks an escape from the ambiguity that so pervades our historical legacy.

American society is more volatile on these matters than

many suspect. Over the previous century and at the beginning of a new one, we have been undergoing waves of contending forms of populism—pendulum swings between totalistic impulses and more open, if less clearly formulated, protean principles. How this psychohistorical struggle will develop we have no way of knowing, but we need hardly give up on ambiguity, or on our capacity to combine it with strongly held ethical principles. There is a real sense in which elements of ambiguity are necessary to our well-being. They certainly are necessary to the well-being of our nation, and of the world.

To live with ambiguity is to accept vulnerability. American aspirations toward superpower invulnerability have troubling parallels in Islamist visions of godly power. Surrendering the dream of invulnerability, more enlightened American leaders could begin to come to terms with the idea that there will always be some danger in our world, that reasonable and measured steps can be taken to limit that danger and combat threats of violence, but that invulnerability is itself a perilous illusion. To cast off that illusion would mean removing the psychological pressure of sustaining a falsified vision of the world, as opposed to taking a genuine place in the real one.

Much of this has to do with accepting the fact that we die, a fact not altered by either superpower militarism or religious fanaticism. A great part of apocalyptic violence is in the service of a vast claim of immortality, a claim that can, in the end, often be sustained only by victimizing large numbers of people. Zealots come to depend upon their mystical, spiritual, or military vision to protect themselves from death, and to provide immortality through killing.

LIMITS

But there is another way. One can achieve alternate forms of larger human continuity—of symbolic immortality—by significant engagement with ideas and communities that extend beyond one's own limited life span. One does not have to destroy life in order to sustain a sense of immortality in one's own group or in the world in general. There is a kind of humane symbolization of immortality inherent in the collective life of culture and history. It has the advantage of being actual rather than illusory, of being lively and renewable.

More broadly, were Americans to reject superpower syndrome, they would also reject a claim to an exclusive American power over life and death. We could then rejoin the world as fellow mortals and in the process rediscover our all too fallible and fragile humanity for the precious gift it is. As Albert Camus, the French writer who struggled with these issues throughout his life put it, to live and to die as humans we need "to refuse to be a god," which means embracing "thought which recognizes limits."

Should we come to such modest human truths, we would recognize the futility of mass violence: its contagion and its ultimate absurdity in the shadow of nuclear weapons. Passionate justifications of apocalyptic violence have distracted much of the world from that deadly absurdity. But if this is a time of hunger for totalism and purification, it is also one of skepticism toward extravagant ideologies and of new explorations of human possibility. Those explorations require, above all, a rejection of omniscience. As Camus also said, "He who does not know everything cannot kill everyone."

NOTES

Introduction: No references

Chapter 1: The Apocalyptic Face-off: No references

Chapter 2: Apocalyptic Violence

Page 13: interpreting Islam: Clifford Geertz, "Which Way to Mecca? Part II," *New York Review of Books*, July 3, 2003.

Page 14: own versions of the apocalyptic: David Cook, "Muslim Apocalyptic and Jihad." *Jerusalem Studies in Arabic and Islam*, 20: 66-104, 1996.

Page 14: "Death-and-rebirth": Joseph Campbell, *Masks of God: Primitive Mythology* (New York: Penguin, 1976), 67.

Page 14: "We believe in the principle": Quoted in Lawrence Wright, "The Man Behind bin Laden," *New Yorker*, Sept. 16, 2002.

Page 14: enraged at his government: Lou Michel and Dan Herbeck, *American Terrorist: Timothy McVeigh and the Oklahoma City Bombing* (New York: Regan Books, 2001). See also Charles B. Strozier, "Apocalyptic Violence and the Politics of Waco," in *The Year 2000: Essays on the End*, eds. Charles B. Strozier and Michael Flynn. (New York: New York University Press, 1997), 97-111.

Page 15: the most apocalyptically murderous volume ever written: Andrew MacDonald [William L. Pierce], *The Turner Diaries* (Hillsboro, WV: National Vanguard Books, 1978), later quotation, iii.

Pages 16: "Allah is [our] goal" and "will cry O Muslim!": Daniel Benjamin and Steven Simon, *The Age of Sacred Terror* (New York: Random House, 2002), 192-93. See also Mark Juergensmeyer, *Terror in the Mind of God: The Global Rise of Religious Violence* (Berkeley: University of California Press, 2000).

Page 16: "the Messiah's coming": Arthur Hertzberg, "Storming Heaven: The Perils of Jewish Messianism," *Reform Judaism*, May 1999.

Page 17: "an agent of the Redemption" and "At the End of Days": Michael Karpin and Ina Friedman, *Murder in the Name of God* (New York: Metropolitan Books, 1998), 44-45, 8.

Page 19: "the world is destroyed and re-created": Mircea Eliade, *Cosmos and History: The Myth of the Eternal Return* (New York: Harper Torchbooks, 1959), 62.

Page 19: "the nature and purpose of history": Bernard McGinn, "The End of the World and the Beginning of Christendom." In *Apocalypse Theory: And the Ends of the World*," ed. Malcolm Bull (Cambridge, Mass.: Blackwell, 1995), 60.

Page 19: "Physical death is not": John Collins, in Bernard McGinn, *Apocalyptic Spirituality* (New York: Paulist Press, 1979), 15.

Page 20: "common denominator": Damian Thompson, *The End of Time* (Hanover, NH: University Press of New England, 1996), 9.

Page 20: Long predating Christianity and Judaism: Norman Cohn, "How Time Acquired a Consummation," in *Apocalypse Theory*, 21.

Page 20: "a decisive opportunity": Christopher Rowland, in *Apocalypse Theory*, 6.

Page 21: "divinely-predetermined pattern" and ""the mother of all Christian theology": McGinn, in *Apocalypse Theory*," 60-61.

Page 23: the guru of the Japanese Aum Shinrikyo cult (and subsequent quotes): Robert Jay Lifton, *Destroying the World to Save It: Aum Shinrikyo, Apocalyptic Violence, and the New Global Terrorism* (New York: Metropolitan Books, 1999), 167.

Page 27: "who could not wait": Gershom Scholem, *The Messianic Idea in Judaism* (New York: Schocken, 1971), 56-57.

Page 27: "messiah-intoxicated Zealots" and "the Messiah would come": Hertzberg, "Storming Heaven."

Page 30: "a hundred corpses . . . an unwritten . . . page of glory": Lucy S. Dawidowicz, *The War Against the Jews, 1933-1945* (New York: Holt, Rinehart & Winston, 1975), 149.

Page 31: "Brothers! . . . I offer you my life" (and subsequent quotes): *The Turner Diaries*, 204, 202, 185.

Page 33: given macabre expression: Nevil Shute, *On the Beach*, 1957 (New York: Ballantine, 1974).

Chapter 3: Century of Excess

Page 36: to medicalize their apocalypse: Robert Jay Lifton, *The Nazi Doctors: Medical Killing and the Psychology of Genocide* (New York: Basic Books, 1986).

Page 37: "the enemy civil population": Charles Webster and Nobel Frankland, *The Strategic Air Offensive Against Germany*, vol. 1 (London: Her Majesty's Stationery Office, 1961), 157.

Page 41: experience of Vice President Harry Truman: Robert Jay Lifton and Greg Mitchell, *Hiroshima in America: Fifty Years of Denial* (New York: Grossett/Putnam, 1995), 143-203.

Page 43: "Everything seemed dark" (and subsequent quotes): Robert Jay Lifton, *Death in Life: Survivors of Hiroshima*, 1968 (Durham: University of North Carolina Press, 1991), 22-23, 29.

Page 43: "searing light" (and subsequent quotes): Robert Jay Lifton, *The Broken Connection: On Death and the Continuity of Life*, 1979 (Washington, DC: American Psychiatric Press, 1996), 370.

Page 44: America's unease or "raw nerve": *Hiroshima in America*, xi-xviii.

Pages 46-47: "atrocity-producing situation" and "What am I doing here?": Robert Jay Lifton, *Home from the War: Vietnam Veterans— Neither Victims nor Executioners* (New York: Simon and Schuster, 1973), 41, 37.

Page 48: "We shall not continue to fight": Courage to Refuse Declaration; Shamai Leibowitz, *Judaism in Favor of Refusal: Ruling over a Hostile Population*. For both documents, www.couragetorefuse.org.

Pages 49-50: "a pitiful, helpless giant," "Vietnam syndrome," and "By God, we've kicked": *Home from the War*, preface and afterword of 1992 edition (Boston: Beacon Press).

Page 51: what the Chinese call "thought reform": Robert Jay Lifton, *Thought Reform and the Psychology of Totalism: A Study of "Brainwashing" in China*, 1961 (Durham: University of North Carolina Press, 1989).

Page 54: "dissolve into piles of mud and bricks": Kang Chao, "The Great Leap," quoted in Lifton, *Revolutionary Immortality: Mao Tse-tung and the Chinese Cultural Revolution* (New York: Random House, 1968), 104.

Pages 54-55: At least twenty million people, "poor and blank," and "there would still be one-half left": Phillip Short, *Mao: A Life* (New York: Henry Holt, 2000), 505, 488-89.

Chapter 4: Aum Shinrikyo—The Threshold Crossed

Page 57: Aum Shinrikyo crossed that threshold: For all aspects of Aum discussed in this chapter, see *Destroying the World to Save It*, including listed references, 36, 47-48, 59-88, 201, 341-44.

Page 70: not scientifically understood: A number of researchers, including Richard Davidson of the University of Wisconsin and Antonio R. Demasio of the University of Iowa, have explored related aspects of brain function. But there is no equivalent in the area we are discussing to the systematic studies that have been done, for instance, in connection with the neurophysiology of posttraumatic stress disorder, as recently summarized by Bessel A. van der Kolk, "The Psychobiology of Posttraumatic Stress Disorder," in *Textbook of Biological Psychiatry*, ed. Jaak Panksepp (New York: Wiley, 2003).

Page 72: "need corpses": Elias Canetti, *Crowds and Power* (New York: Viking, 1962), 443.

Chapter 5: Bin Laden and al–Qaeda—*"I Envision Saladin Coming Out of the Clouds"*

Page 74: "Osama never interpreted Islam": Rohan Gunaratna, *Inside Al Qaeda: Global Network of Terror* (New York: Columbia University Press, 2002), 89.

Page 75: "Our duty is to put an end"; "America thinks it is strong"; "Our duty is to struggle": Roland Jacquard, *In the Name of Osama bin Laden: Global Terrorism and the bin Laden Brotherhood* (Durham: Duke University Press, 2002), 101, 104-05.

Page 75: "a defense of the worldwide Islamic community": John L. Esposito, *Unholy War. Terror in the Name of Islam* (New York: Oxford University Press, 2002), 21. See also Gilles Kepel, *Jihad: The Trail of Political Islam* (Cambridge, Mass.: Harvard University Press, 2002).

Page 75: One observer believes that: Gunaratna, 84-94.

Page 76: "that Muhammad and his earliest followers" (and subsequent quotes): Cook, "Muslim Apocalyptic and Jihad."

Page 77: "We return from the lesser jihad": Esposito, 62-63.

Page 77-78: "the rule of God's Religion" ... "far enemy": Benjamin and Simon, 78.

Page 78: "striving in the path of God" (and subsequent quotations): David C. Rapoport, "Sacred Terror: A Contemporary Example from Islam," in *Origins of Terrorism: Psychologies, Ideologies, Theologies, States of Mind*, ed. Walter Reich (New York: Cambridge University Press, 1990), 110-11, 118.

Page 79: Qutb wrote powerfully about *Jahiliyya* ... "kingdom of heaven on earth": Benjamin and Simon, 64-65, 68.

Page 79-80: "the Emir of Jihad" ... "will reign again": Esposito, 7.

Pages 82-83: the "Zionist-crusader alliance" ... "faith in Allah": Benjamin and Simon, 141, 149-50.

Page 84: "a broad movement of Islamic militancy": Jason Burke, "Powell Doesn't Know Who He's up Against," *The Observer* [London], Feb. 9, 2003.

Page 84: who is "impressionistic": Ahmed Rashid, *Taliban: Militant Islam, Oil and Fundamentalism in Central Asia* (New Haven: Yale University Press, 2000).

Page 85: "envision[ed] Saladin coming out of the clouds": Ken Ringle, "The Crusaders' Giant Footprints: After a Millennium, Their Mark Remains," *Washington Post*, Oct. 23, 2001.

Page 85: "bin Laden and his companions": Kepel, 16.

Page 86: issue a defiant message: Osama bin Laden's tape recording received on Feb. 11, 2003 (http://abcnews.go.com/sections/world/dailynews/binladen_transcript030211.html).

Page 86: Islamist terrorists enter into a sacred drama (and subsequent quotes): Hassan Mneimneh and Kanan Makiya, "Manual for a Small 'Raid,'" *New York Review of Books*, Jan. 17, 2002.

Page 88: "A civilian passenger attempting to resist": Ruthven, 37.

Page 88: "You will be soon, with God's permission": Mneimneh and Makiya.

Chapter 6: The Terrorist Dynamic

Page 97: Little boys and girls: Nicholas D. Kristof, "Kids with Bombs," *New York Times*, April 5, 2002.

Page 98: far from alone in his conviction: Karpin and Friedman, 105-06.

Page 103: "the followers of Satan": Benjamin and Simon, 164.

Page 104: "What he says and does": David Hirst, *Toronto Globe and Mail*, Oct. 9, 2001.

Page 105: "what the United States tastes today": Osama bin Laden statement of Oct. 7, 2001, quoted by Michael Scott Doran in "Somebody Else's Civil War," Evatt Foundation publication, Jan. 23, 2003.

Page 105: "They hate us as people hate a bad God": Denis Johnson, quoted in "Dispatches," *New Yorker*, Sept. 24, 2001.

Chapter 7: A Superpower's "War on Terrorism"

Page 109: "this conflict was begun": Bob Woodward, *Bush at War* (New York: Simon and Schuster, 2002), 67. With the exception of "war fever," remaining quotations in the chapter are from this book, pp. 48-49, 60, 67, 73, 78, 81, 83, 96, 224.

Page 114: Woolsey and This Fourth World War CNN: (http://www.cnn.com/2003/us/04/03/sprj.irq.woolsey.world.war/)

Chapter 8: Apocalyptic America

Page 118: "a very evil and wicked religion," "I'm also under orders," and "The king of kings and the lord of lords," *New Republic*, April 21, 2003.

Page 118: "predominant creed" . . . "not quite *uncompulsory*, either": David Frum, *The Right Man: The Surprise Presidency of George W. Bush* (New York: Random House, 2003), 17, 4-5.

Page 119: "We have no king but Jesus": Transcript of Attorney General John Ashcroft's speech at Bob Jones University, May 8, 1999, abcnews.com, Jan. 12, 2001 (http://abcnews.go.com/sections/politics/DailyNews/ashcroft_bjutranscript010112.html).

Page 119: "only aid terrorists": "Ashcroft: Critics of New Terror Measures Undermine Effort," cnn.com./u.s. Dec. 7, 2001 (http://www.cnn.com/2001/US/12/06/inv.ashcroft.hearing/).

Pages 119-120: "A great opportunity," "This is what my presidency," "I'm in the Lord's hands" (and subsequent quotes): Woodward, 46, 102, 286, 339.

Page 120: aggressive taunting of enemies: Steve Holland, "Bush Taking Heat for 'Bring Them on' Remark," July 3, 2003 (http://story.news.yahoo.com/news?tmpl=story&u=/nm/20030703/pl_nm/iraq_bush_dc).

Page 121: "God told me to strike": "Antichrist Claims God Talked to Him, Told Him to Attack al Qaida, and Saddam," in *Ha'aretz* June 26, 2003 (http://www.indybay.org/news/2003/06/1622523.php).

Page 122: "lift the curtain and allow the enemies": Scott Simon, "Reflections on the Events of September 11, 2001," Annual Parker Lecture (http://www.ucc.org/ocinc/parker/simon.htm).

Page 123: Millions of Americans hold aspects of such a worldview: Charles B. Strozier, *Apocalypse: On the Psychology of Fundamentalism in America* (Boston: Beacon Press, 1994).

Page 123: "holy war": Richard Slotkin, *Regeneration through Violence* (Middletown, Conn.: Wesleyan University Press, 1973), 84.

Page 124: "We will export death and violence": Woodward, 352.

Chapter 9: Superpower Vulnerability

Page 126: "'Tis our true policy": *Bartlett's Familiar Quotations*, Justin Kaplan, general ed. (New York: Little Brown, 1992), 336.

Page 126: "All the armies of Europe": Roy P. Basler, ed. *The Collected Works of Abraham Lincoln* (New Brunswick, NJ: Rutgers University Press, 1953, 1972, 1990), vol. 1, 109.

Page 127: "A course almost without limits": Quoted in Tony Tanner, introduction to *Herman Melville, the Confidence Man* (New York: Oxford University Press, 1989), xvi.

Page 127: "a double-edged sword": subtitle of Seymour Martin Lipset's study, *American Exceptionalism* (New York: Norton, 1996); "utopian moralists": 63, and subsequent Hofstadter quote, p. 18.

Page 127: "Arcadian image of the New World" (and subsequent quotes): Slotkin, 38, 5, 34.

Page 128: "shell game of identity": Tanner, xxxiii.

Page 130: Every nuclear-age president: Lifton and Mitchell, *Hiroshima in America*, 211-22.

Page 132: The pattern is ominous: Robert Jay Lifton, "Illusions of the Second Nuclear Age," *World Policy Journal*, vol. 18, no. 1, Spring 2001; Jonathan Schell, "The Growing Nuclear Peril," June 24, 2002, and "The Case Against the War," March 3, 2003 (both in *The Nation*); and Bill Keller, "The Thinkable," *New York Times Magazine*, May 4, 2003.

Page 134: "My ideal for the perfect number of nuclear-weapons states is one": Keller, 101.

Chapter 10: Americans as Survivors

Page 137: the psychology of the survivor: Robert Jay Lifton, "The Concept of the Survivor," in *The Future of Immortality: And Other Essays for a Nuclear Age* (New York: Basic Books, 1987), 231-43.

Page 139: studies of trauma symptoms: Sandro Galea et al., "Psychological Sequelae of the September 11 Terrorist Attacks in New York City," *New England Journal of Medicine*, vol. 346, March 28, 2002, 982-87; and Jennifer Stuber et al., "Determinants of Counseling for Children in Manhattan After the September 11 Attacks," *Psychiatric Services*, vol. 53, July 2002, 815-22.

Page 142: "zones of sadness": Term used by Charles Strozier and Michael Flynn. See Strozier, "The World Trade Center Disaster and the Apocalyptic," *Psychoanalytic Dialogues*, 12:361-80, 2002; and "From Ground Zero: Apocalyptic Violence and the World Trade Center Disaster, in *Dialogues on Terror: Patients and Their Psychoanalysts. Special issue of Psychoanalysis and Psychotherapy*, vol. 20, no. 2, Fall 2003.

Page 146: The members of Company C: *Home from the War*, 41-65.

Page 148: "he looked and sounded like the hunted": Frum, 119.

Page 150: intention to hijack planes: "What Bush Knew Before September 11," cbsnews.com. May 17, 2002 (http://www.cbsnews.com/stories/2002/05/16/attack/main509294.shtml). This report also mentions a study issued two years before September 11, which suggested that al–Qaeda suicide bombers "could crash-land an aircraft packed with high explosives . . . into the Pentagon, the headquarters of the Central Intelligence Agency, or the White House."

Page 150: "The Pentagon could not defend the Pentagon": Elaine Scarry, presentation to Harvard University Group on Mass Violence, Feb. 7, 2003.

Page 151-152: "Some Republicans on the Hill": *Time* magazine, special issue commemorating September 11, 2001.

Pages 151-152: "very, very, very eerie" . . . "no question about that":
  Woodward, 69, 73, 145.

Page 153: "a spike in recruitment": David Johnston with Don van
  Natta Jr., "U.S. Officials See Signs of a Revived Al Qaeda," *New
  York Times*, May 17, 2003.

Page 153: parable for such blunted perception: James Carroll,
  "Watching the War with Both Eyes," *Boston Globe*, Feb. 25, 2003.

Page 155: "deep regret and sympathy " . . . "an atmosphere that is
  encouraging terrorism": Graham Jones, "Divisions Evident in
  Islamic Mideast, N. Africa," Sept. 25, 2001 (http://www.cnn.com/
  2001/WORLD/meast/09/24/arab.standpoints.)

Page 156: "a big organizing idea" and "was encountering": Frum, 274.

Chapter 11: Stages of Response

Page 161: twenty-three known cases . . . for about five months: James M.
  Hughes and Julie Louise Gerberding, "Anthrax Bioterrorism:
  Lessons Learned and Future Directions," *Emerging Infectious Diseases
  Journal*, Center for Disease Control, vol. 8, no. 10, Oct. 2002; and
  Spencer S. Hsu, "Senators Return to Hart Building: Offices Reopen
  After 96-Day Anthrax Quarantine," *Washington Post*, Jan. 23, 2002.

Page 162: *invisible contamination: Death in Life*, 57-102.

Page 163: sense of *futurelessness*: Robert Jay Lifton and Richard Falk,
  *Indefensible Weapons: The Political and Psychological Case Against
  Nuclearism* (New York: Basic Books, 1982), 67 ff, 80 ff.

Page 164: These doubts have been reinforced: Gary Hart and
  Warren B. Rudman, Co-Chairs, Stephen E. Flynn, Project
  Director, "America—Still Unprepared, Still in Danger." Report
  of an independent task force sponsored by the Council on For-
  eign Relations, Oct. 2002. The report declares that "A year after
  September 11, America remains dangerously unprepared to pre-
  vent and respond to a catastrophic terrorist attack on U.S. soil."
  Hart and Rudman had also co-chaired an earlier report, dated
  March 15, 2001, for the US Commission on National Security, in
  which they declared that preparations for a likely attack on
  American soil were "fragmented and inadequate."

Page 165: "sleepwalking through history": "We Stand Passively Mute."

Statement by Senator Robert Byrd to US Senate, Feb. 14, 2003 (http://www.scoop.co.nz/mason/stories/WO0302/S00153.htm).

Chapter 12: Fluid World Control

Page 173: "planned (or as it seems, largely unplanned)" . . . "sign on to support it": William B. Pfaff, "The World According to Bush," *Boston Globe*, April 19, 2003.

Page 174: "intended to mark the official emergence": Jay Bookman, "The President's Real Goal in Iraq," *Atlanta Journal-Constitution*, Sept. 29, 2002.

Page 174: National Security Strategy statement: The National Security Strategy of the United States of America, the White House, Sept. 2002, US Department of State, International Information Programs.

Page 177: "Defense becomes offense": James Carroll, "Wanton Cruelty," *Boston Globe*, Oct. 29, 2002.

Page 179: "ultimate national security" . . . "absolute security": David C. Hendrickson, "America's Dangerous Quest for Absolute Security," *World Policy Journal*, Fall 2002, 9.

Page 184: completely forged and falsified documents: Joby Warrick, "U.N. Says Evidence Was Faked: Report Calls into Question U.S. Claims of Nuclear Program," *Washington Post*, March 8, 2003.

Page 184: During the 1980s, studies showed: *Indefensible Weapons*, 48-56.

Page 184: fears of environmental catastrophe: Strozier and Lifton, unpublished manuscript on nuclear fear.

Chapter 13: Stepping Out of the Syndrome

Page 197: possibility of evolution and change: Geertz, "Which Way to Mecca? Part II."

Page 197: a version of the self: Robert Jay Lifton, *The Protean Self: Human Resilience in an Age of Fragmentation*, 1993 (Chicago: University of Chicago Press, 1999).

Page 198: elements of ambiguity are necessary: David Tracy, *Plurality and Ambiguity: Hermeneutics, Religion, Hope* (Chicago: University of Chicago Press, 1987).

Page 199-200: "to refuse to be a god," "thought which," and "He who does not": Albert Camus, *The Rebel* (New York: Knopf, 1954), 261, 273.

ACKNOWLEDGMENTS

While this book is concerned with contemporary history, it draws upon ideas evolved over a professional lifetime. A truly extraordinary contribution to the work was made by Charles Strozier, close colleague and equally close friend of many years. Our continuous dialogue on practically everything culminated in a specific dialogue on the content and sequence of the book, from beginning to end.

I learned much from discussions of these demanding issues that took place in the Harvard University Group on Mass Violence and in the Wellfleet Psychohistory Group.

Tom Engelhardt brought his unparalleled editorial imagination to bear on every concept and argument of the book—insistently, brilliantly, movingly.

Carl Bromley has been a thoughtful and energizing taskmaster in overseeing the project for Nation Books.

I am grateful to the Foundation for Psychocultural Research, and to its president, Robert Lemelson, for supporting the overall project. I wish also to thank the Simons Foundation and its president, Jennifer Allen Simons, for earlier research support.

Allison Stieber, my assistant at the Cambridge Health Alliance, did valuable research, coordinated a great deal, and skillfully prepared the manuscript.

From its origins, Betty Jean Lifton has conveyed to me her sense of the project's importance, while constantly contributing to it with her own ideas and interpretations, and providing the love that made it possible.

973.931
L   Lifton, Robert Jay.
          Superpower syndrome.

                              $12.95

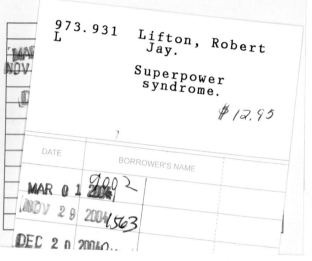

973.931
L   Lifton, Robert
          Jay.
          Superpower
          syndrome.
                              $12.95

DATE	BORROWER'S NAME	
MAR 0 1 2002		
NOV 2 9 2004 1563		
DEC 2 0 2010		